SNATCHED
FROM THE
FIRE

by
Patricia Amis

CCB Publishing
British Columbia, Canada

Snatched from the Fire

Library and Archives Canada Cataloguing in Publication

Amis, Patricia, 1968-
Snatched from the fire / written by Patricia Amis – 3rd ed.
ISBN 978-1-926585-87-1
I. Title.
PS3601.M58S63 2010   813'.6   C2010-903797-9

Cover image, *Heart on Fire*, © Laconic Software is reproduced with permission.

Publisher: CCB Publishing
British Columbia, Canada
www.ccbpublishing.com

ACKNOWLEDGMENTS

I would like to first thank my heavenly father for allowing me to know who he is, and what he represents. I am also thankful for the creator of our universe who allowed his Holy Spirit to overshadow my life, which set me free. I am thankful that JESUS CHRIST died for our sins so that we may have a right to the tree of life. I would like to also give thanks to my mother, Rachel Smith, who experienced many sleepless nights while praying for me; Aunt Doris Smith (AKA "Billie Jean") who always stepped in when I needed her; my sister Denise Smith, who fought many battles for me when I didn't even know it; my beautiful, intelligent daughter, Rachel Fenton; and my son, who always stayed by my side and believed in me, even when it seemed as if I had given up on hope. I would like to express a royal Thank You to my husband Reginald who is my best friend, who remained supportive while I finished this project. Many more thanks to all of my associates in the universe. Words could never describe how much I appreciate all of your support, so I will sum it up and say "I love you."

PREFACE

Just because we cannot see it, does not mean that it will not affect us. Danger always resides within the darkness, when there is no light present in order to manifest hope. Sometimes we make decisions not realizing that there exists a lurking, dangerous fire that you become a part of and that commands to be a part of you. Some people notice the fire in your life, and dare not to expose it. The individuals who have no knowledge concerning the mystery of the camouflages are seated in the safety zone of life. No matter where you run or where you hide, the fire finds you. Once you decide that you do not want to be a part of this dangerous fire, it decides not to take "no" for an answer. The fire will affect every area of your life adversely, once you reject it. Sabrina never knew that the fire was real. She never detected the camouflages that were presented before her. She never believed in the path regarding the truth that sets individuals free. Sabrina became a part of the fire, and is snatched away into a marvelous light of freedom by a man that she always dreamed about . . .

PART I

It was a cold morning on September 19, 1974. While looking out of the window, I noticed the leaves briskly falling off the tree which was located at the corner of the pink and white house where we resided. I was getting ready to celebrate my seventh birthday with my family. The house had the smell of collard greens, fried chicken, and pastries being cooked. The colorful balloons were stuck to the freshly painted walls of the living room. Pink and white streamers were twisted high above the cathedral ceilings. A long banner was stretched across the room which read "Happy 7th Birthday Sabrina." My birthday cake was carefully placed on the oblong table, adjacent to my mother's bedroom. It was apparent that my mother was enjoying herself while preparing for the party.

Finally, after hours of my mother preparing for this festive occasion, the doorbell rang. It was my aunt, my mother's sister Carey, who lived upstairs from us. Carey was the owner of the house. Through her actions and speech, she always reminded my mother that she was doing us a favor by renting the downstairs apartment to us. When Aunt Carey came down to our apartment, she always appeared as if she was expecting to hear unfortunate news about myself or my sister – she always wore a shrewd smile and her face appeared almost mystical.

Well, Aunt Carey was in her early forties and she sported a short Afro hairstyle. She seemed quite happy with her profession, working with the local Community Center. She was married to Skinner. I always overheard her dictating plans to the family. When Aunt Carey became emotionally out of control, Skinner was always able to calm her down somehow.

"Hello, everybody," stated Aunt Carey as she entered the living room of our four room apartment. Aunt Carey had on a plaid polyester shirt, with a pair of matching pants. She had on a pair of platform shoes, which she seemed to be struggling to walk in.

"Hi, Sabrina, Happy Birthday" exclaimed Aunt Carey, as she hugged me closely. "Sabrina, we are all going to have a nice time today. All of your cousins are going to come downstairs and celebrate with you. Would you like that?" she questioned as she pinched my right cheek.

"That sounds like fun," I replied. Before I knew it, the living room became filled with more relatives. Although Aunt Carey's kids were older than us, I was happy to have them around, although they didn't feel the same way.

Aunt Carey's kids seemed to be having a great time telling jokes and watching the black and white television which had a coat hanger controlling the reception. They seemed to be enjoying the motions of flipping back and forth to the only four channels on the television that we had access to. This gathering did not seem like my birthday party. It began to feel like more of an invasion. My little sister Dana and I were quietly seated on the plaid striped couch until my cousin,

Gabriella, broke the monotony.

"So, little girl, it's time for your birthday party. We finally get to eat up your food, instead of you eating up our food." Everybody laughed hysterically. Gabriella was the leader of the pack of her other three siblings. She was like E.F. Hutton. When she spoke, everybody listened. Gabriella was at least five years older than me. I remember on one occasion when I went upstairs to my Aunt Carey's house. The house seemed quite dreary, but I could smell the aroma, on that particular day, of fresh fish being fried. I abruptly opened the door and my cousin, Gabriella, was standing there with her two friends. The vocals of Stevie Wonder consumed the entire living room. She had on a red flare shirt and a matching blouse. The wooden clogs that she had on accented her entire outfit. The look on her face frightened me. I was intimidated.

"So, Sabrina, why did you come up here?" she asked. "Oh, let me guess," she abruptly stated, "you must be hungry." Her two friends began laughing hysterically. "She only comes up here to get a meal," exclaimed Gabriella. "She's so greedy. Watch this," she screamed as she stared at me with the evil eye. "Come here, Sabrina, are you hungry?"

"Yes," I eagerly replied as she led me into the kitchen. Gabriella began to aggressively stuff bread into my mouth.

"Eat this, you're so greedy," she screamed as she continued stuffing the bread into my mouth. My Aunt Carey stood there, with a smirk on her face, and did not say a word. Gabriella's two friends laughed. I wanted to cry, but before I could, Uncle Skinner came into the kitchen.

"What's going on?" he exclaimed. When he realized that I was being emotionally abused, he stepped in. "Leave the girl alone," he stated.

"She's so greedy," yelled Gabriella. "The next time I'm going to make her eat dog food." As Uncle Skinner led me downstairs to the apartment where I resided, I held down my head, vowing never to be hungry whenever I was around my cousin Gabriella.

The time was drawing near for my birthday party to end. My family cheerfully sang the Happy Birthday song to me. The lyrics of the Jackson 5's ABC song engulfed the living room where we were all seated. It was getting late; I was tired. Aunt Carey and her children packed piles of cake and food into shopping bags and proceeded to go upstairs. I was happy that the day was over.

It was a new day. I woke up with a renewed feeling of being seven years old. By the look on my mother's face, she must have done too much work yesterday preparing for my birthday party, and entertaining the family, so I thought. My sister, Dana, and I were quietly sitting on the living room sofa, when my mother stumbled out of the bathroom into the hallway.

"I don't know what's wrong with me," she stated. "I'm not feeling too well." My sister, Dana, and I ran out into the hallway and stood next to our mother. In the past, my mother had had episodes when she did not feel well. I remember, on several occasions, when Dana and I went to the emergency room with her. When our mommy fell ill, I always ran into the other room and left Dana there with her. This time I was determined to stay by my mother's side. As my mother stood in the hallway, she began to appear as if she were going to pass out. My sister, Dana, and I stood there, wondering what would happen next. Almost suddenly, my Aunt Carey appeared at the top of the steps, as my mother helplessly leaned on the banister at the bottom of the steps.

"What's wrong with you?" Carey screamed as she put her hands on her hips.

"I don't know," my mother wearily replied. "I'm not

feeling too well," she stated as she attempted to catch her breath.

"There's nothing wrong with you," my Aunt Carey screamed, as if my mother had highly offended her. Aunt Carey began to yell at my mother as if she were a helpless stranger. "You're crazy, there's nothing wrong with you. I'm tired of you creating these illnesses." Aunt Carey was yelling so loudly that Uncle Skinner came onto the scene in order to see what the problem was. Uncle Skinner was a black man, with a high yellow complexion. He was tall and thin. Uncle Skinner always sported farmer's pants and construction boots. I believe that he was a construction worker by trade.

"Baby, why are you yelling at her like that?" Uncle Skinner questioned, as my sister and I stood helplessly at the side of our mother.

"No, Skinner, I'm tired of her with these 'I don't feel good' episodes. There's nothing wrong with her. She's just crazy. She needs to go into the psych-ward," Aunt Carey screamed. Although I didn't understand what was happening, it made me upset and sad to hear her speaking to my mother like that.

"Just leave her alone," stated Uncle Skinner, as he grabbed Aunt Carey by the hand. "Sis," he yelled as he walked down the steps towards my mother, "I'm going to take you to the hospital; let's go."

My sister, Dana, and I sat patiently, as we waited for my mother to return from the hospital. My mother's youngest sister, Aunt Debbie, came over and read children's books to us. The rooster clock calmly ticked on the kitchen wall. As time passed on, it seemed as if the ticking of the clock became louder and louder. After about five hours, Uncle Skinner returned with my mother.

"She's okay," he breathlessly stated. "She will need plenty of rest." I always wondered why my mother came home from the hospital with no diagnosis. After all, at least in my mind, the hospital was the place where you went in order to get help, or was it?

The month of December was quickly approaching. The thick snow on the ground proudly announced that the holiday season was near. On this particular evening, my mother's father came over to our house in order to visit. He was a dark skinned man, with a clean-shaved head. He smoked a sweet-smelling pipe, and talked loudly. He always had the pleasure of burning holes into our rugs when he "missed the garbage can" while emptying the ashes from his pipe.

He constantly talked about our step-grandmother who lived with him in Brooklyn. He always spoke about her being such a dedicated Pentecostal minister in the church, and how she always prayed for people. She was a beautician and served as a part-time volunteer prison worker. She was the primary individual who believed that David Berkowitz, also known as The Son of Sam serial killer, and the 44 caliber killer, had a right to be free. She believed that his killing sprees were a result of the demons attacking and harassing him. She believed that he was innocent. My grandmother visited him in prison every week, and helped him to learn Bible verses. His psychiatrist told everyone that "David Berkowitz was ecstatic, radiant, and quoting scripture right and left" after each time Grandma left his presence. Although David Berkowitz was a serial killer, she believed that he was a true apostle of The Lord. Her face was all over the local newspapers, because of her *"spiritual ties"* to David Berkowitz.

Although we didn't see her very often, for some strange reason the image of her face was "stuck in my head." It almost frightened me. The image of "minister" that my grandfather created of his wife did not match the image of how *I* perceived her.

"Hey, Sabrina," exclaimed my grandfather. "How are you doing?" he asked as he dusted the snow off of his heavy work boots. My grandfather always had a proverb to give me when he visited. "Sabrina, remember this," he stated as he softly chucked, "when you get a job and feel like staying home, remember you'd better go, because you need the job, the job doesn't need you." My grandfather sat and spoke with my mother for at least five hours. Finally, he left in order in order to go home.

In my dream on that particular night, I saw the face of my grandmother. She was sitting at a table. Someone was sitting across from her, but I could not recognize the face. I tried to squint, hoping to gain revelation of the other person, but I couldn't. My grandmother began to speak. I could not make out the words that she was uttering. My grandmother pulled out a deck of cards, and began shuffling. She split the deck in two, and began turning the cards over, one by one, as she was speaking. The first card that I noticed was a card with two angels. One was black and one was white. The next card that I saw was a card with a black beast on it, and the words at the bottom read "Death." There were other strange cards that I saw, but they were blurred. As my grandmother turned over the next card, I abruptly woke up out of my sleep. My mother had just knocked on the bedroom door. After all, it was around the holidays and my mother wanted to make everything perfect for us. She had just finished putting up the tree, and we were ready to put the decorations on the tree. It was a beautiful morning. While we were putting up the tree, there was a knock at the door. Dana and I eagerly ran towards the front door. I looked through the glass window pane, and noticed that *it was her* – my grandmother. She had two shopping bags in her hands, filled with perfectly wrapped Christmas gifts for us. We opened the door, in anticipation of receiving a friendly greeting.

"Hello, Grandma," I reluctantly stated.

"Hi, Sabrina," she abruptly replied. "These gifts are for you and Dana," she stated as she lunged the shopping bags at us. "I hope that you enjoy these gifts. Oh, Sabrina, I especially hope that you enjoy your gifts," she stated as she mysteriously glanced at me. "You will be a lucky child if you even ever make it out of high school." She immediately turned away and walked out of sight, into the snow-covered hills.

Many years quickly passed by. My sister Dana and I had just received the news that we were moving out of Aunt Carey's house into City Housing. Although we were moving into unfamiliar territory, I was happy to move away from Aunt Carey and her kids. We didn't have to worry about milk and eggs missing from our refrigerator, ever again.

Once we finally got settled into our new environment, it wasn't so bad after all. By this time, I was twelve years old. I met a lot of different people, and quickly adjusted to the change. Dana and I became friends with many children who lived in the projects that had fathers who were part of their lives. Although I had heard about my father, Mr. Barnes, I did not know who he was. Over a period of about five years, I painfully repressed the fears and insecurities of hearing about, and not knowing, my father. At this point in my life, just turning thirteen years old, I longed to meet the man who was responsible for helping my mother bring me into this world. One day, while I was sitting in the living room with my mother, I decided to question her concerning the whereabouts of my father.

"You know, Mom," I softly stated, with a gleam in my eyes, "a lot of these kids over here in the projects don't have their fathers living with them, but I often hear them talking about how they spent the weekend with their father or how they just got off the phone with their father."

"Yeah," shouted my younger sister Dana, "They talk about spending time with their fathers, and how they showed their fathers their latest report cards. We want to know who our father is too." Well, the look on my mother's face was more than surprising. She appeared to have been in shock concerning our request.

"Well," my mother replied, "you can call him if you want to," she stated as she peered out of the living room window, pretending to be preoccupied by the crowd standing in the front of the building. "He works down at the County Hospital, over there in Brooklyn," she stated as she looked towards the front door. My mother proceeded to briskly walk into the bedroom nearby. She returned, holding a piece of paper containing the telephone number of my father. She reluctantly handed me the withered piece of paper which read, "number for Barnes, 33-548-1281." I eagerly ran over to the telephone and frantically dialed my father's telephone number. My sister Dana eagerly stood behind me and waited.

"Hello, this is Mr. Barnes speaking." As the man on the other side of the telephone completed his sentence, I quickly hung up the phone.

"What happened?" asked my sister Dana, as she quickly sat down on the couch.

"It was him, it was him," I exclaimed in a loud voice. "I was scared, so I hung up the phone."

"Try again," my sister Dana desperately pleaded.

"Okay, let's do it," I cheerfully responded. I began to feel butterflies in my stomach, as I proceeded to dial the number. My head began to feel light, and my fingertips began to tingle.

"Hello," abruptly stated the man on the other end of the telephone.

"Hello, this is Sabrina, Rona's daughter, Dana's sister, your daughter from Staten Island." There was brief pause of about two minutes. "Hello, Mr. Barnes?"

"Yes," he cheerfully replied. Mr. Barnes finally broke the monotony. "Hello, who is this?"

"It's Sabrina, your daughter from Staten Island," I excitedly replied.

"Sabrina?"

"Yes," I replied.

"Hi, how have you been? Are you and your sister okay?"

"We're still living," I replied, "but we're better off now that we have found you. Dana and I would like to see you."

"That would be really nice. I would like to see you both also," he nervously replied. I proceeded to give Mr. Barnes our address. I was so excited. Dana danced a jig, as I negotiated a date and time for Mr. Barnes to meet us.

"Okay, Sabrina, I will come and spend some time with you and Dana on Saturday. I will call you around 10 o'clock, when I'm on my way." I abruptly hung up the telephone and told my mom the good news.

"Hey, Mom, I just got off of the telephone with him," I shouted. "He's coming to get us next Saturday. Hey, Mom," I excitedly shouted, "do you have any stories to tell about my father? I mean, what type of person is he?"

"He is a good person, but he did have his faults. I can remember when he was ordered to appear in court, in order to pay child support payments for you and Dana. He was there all dressed in his fancy suit and hat and also with who I would call a special guest, sitting in the courtroom," she stated as she glanced at Dana and I.

"Who was the guest?" I anxiously questioned.

"Well, this is how the story began," she replied. "There was a woman that he was dating after we broke up, who had this brother who was a stoned-cold alcoholic. Your father had him tell a big lie in the courtroom. He told the judge that I was his girlfriend and that he fathered the both of you, although the paternity tests came out positive, proving that Mr. Barnes is *really* your father. The man in the courtroom was 'drunk as a skunk' and lied about everything that he was asked."

I remember one day last year, my mother was talking on the telephone to Aunt Carey, regarding the past conflict between her and my father.

"Yeah, he brought that old drunk brother of his girlfriend into the courtroom," my mother exclaimed. "I couldn't believe it. You could smell the beer on his breath before you got to the door," she stated as she began to frantically laugh. "I was so shocked when he told the judge that he was my boyfriend for fifteen years. Oh, and the best part is, when he asked the drunk man how often he had visited me at my house, he told the judge that he was at my house all of the time. I wanted to smack Barnes because he probably paid the man to tell all of those lies to the judge, and you know, Barnes had the nerve to be laughing hysterically while the man told his lies. Barnes should be ashamed of himself. The judge asked him if I had any distinctive marks on my body, and I know that Mr. Barnes told him what to say. I mean, it was awful what he did. The stupid girlfriend told the judge that I dated her drunken brother, and that she saw us at her house many times."

It was obvious that whatever my father had done in the past to hurt her still bothered her in some way. In many ways, I did not blame her. I continued to listen to her story.

"He never paid the child support," she exclaimed.

I was so happy. I could not describe the way that I was feeling, as a result of speaking with my father for the very first time. Part of me was experiencing happiness, but the greater part of me was feeling fearful. Many questions began to overcrowd my mind. What if Mr. Barnes didn't like me?

What if Mr. Barnes didn't like the way that I looked? What if I did not meet all of his expectations?

Saturday quickly approached. Dana and I were getting dressed, and practicing what we were going to say to our father during our first meeting. Dana and I were dressed to kill, so we thought. I had on a green and red turtleneck, with a pair of white tennis sneakers. I sported the latest hairstyle, two cornrows and a bang which accented my forehead. Dana sported a pair of black penny-loafers. After Dana and I stood on the balcony of the project apartment where we resided, for about twenty minutes, we noticed a big white Cadillac drive up to the building. The excitement that I was feeling made me feel like I was waiting for Santa Claus to arrive. I was so happy. The phone rang. Dana eagerly ran inside to the telephone, and answered it.

"Hello," Dana cheerfully stated.

"Hi, this is Mr. Barnes. Come on down; I'm in the front of the building."

"Okay," responded my sister Dana. Dana and I quickly kissed our mother goodbye, and dashed down the seven flights of stairs. We briskly walked out of the building towards the vehicle that Mr. Barnes was seated in. As we got closer, I noticed the cheerful look on his face. He had the skin tone of caramel candy. Mr. Barnes had a head full of white hair, which resembled cotton. He also had a salt and pepper moustache and beard. As we got closer to the car, Mr. Barnes stepped out of his luxurious vehicle. Mr. Barnes had on a three-piece suit with suspenders. The bowtie that he wore accented the alligator-skin shoes that he had on. He was dressed to kill, for real. As he reached out his arms in order to hug me, the brick-cell phone in his vehicle made a buzzing sound.

"Hi, Sabrina and Dana," he gleefully shouted as he kissed

and hugged us both. "You can get into the car. Sabrina, sit in the front." Although I was happy to meet my father, I was also feeling nervous. The vehicle was luxurious and its leather seats clung to my body. The fresh smell of leather engulfed my nostrils. The music that was playing on the radio soothed my soul.

"So, girls, how is school?" Mr. Barnes asked us, as he quickly glanced into the rear-view mirror at my sister Dana.

"It's fine. I'm actually doing well," I replied.

"I'm doing okay," Dana reluctantly shouted.

"I am so happy to see you both. I'm going to take you out to eat breakfast. Where would you like to go?"

"The pancake house," we both shouted. As we approached the pancake house, I noticed a waitress standing outside, preparing to greet the three of us. We all got out of the vehicle and entered into the restaurant.

"Table for three," Mr. Barnes shouted. It was obvious that he was accustomed to the best treatment that one had to offer, while dining. We sat at a large booth. A beautiful arrangement of pink daisies was placed in the center of the table. Three large glasses of iced-water were placed at the corners of each of the placemats. Decorative napkins were neatly placed on the table, along with the utensils.

We all sat down at the table. Dana and I quickly glanced at each other, as we commenced to give Mr. Barnes our undivided attention. I began to feel as if this were all a dream. Actually sitting down face to face with my father. We all sat quietly for about five minutes, hoping that someone would break the monotony until Mr. Barnes shouted, "So girls, how are you both *really* doing in school?" he asked as if we were actually drop-outs, withholding vital information. One of us had to speak up first. It wasn't going to be Dana, so I spoke up.

"Well," I reluctantly replied, "it is okay."

"How are your grades?"

"I'm on the honor roll," I cheerfully replied.

"What about you, Dana?" he questioned as he stared her in the eyes.

"My grades are okay. I'm just waiting to get out of school so that I could run the country." We all chuckled. Finally, the waiter appeared.

"What are we having?" he asked.

"Give the girls anything on the menu that they ask for." I could not believe what Mr. Barnes was saying. We actually had the opportunity to order whatever we wanted. It was just like the episodes from the movies or television. After glancing over the menus that were carefully taped to the tables, I was ready to order.

"I'm going to have three pancakes, bacon, and three scrambled eggs," I stated.

"Give me the same," shouted Dana to the waiter.

"And you, sir?" questioned the waiter.

"I will have bacon, fried hard, two scrambled eggs soft, toast and coffee. Also, bring out two orange juices for the girls."

"Thank you, your food will be right out," stated the waiter.

"So, girls," stated Mr. Barnes, as he casually put his arm around me, "I know that you have many questions. There's no need to feel bad, because I'm going to be part of your lives from now on. I've always loved the both of you." Mr. Barnes was obviously having a difficult time expressing himself. "I've been really busy, but I never meant to hurt you girls. Are you both willing to get to know me?"

"Yes," we both anxiously replied.

"Just for the record, I just want you both to know that my father was an Irish man. You both have Irish blood running through your veins. You are both *endowed* with the luck of the Irish." We all chuckled. Although Mr. Barnes expressed an interest in being part of my life, I still felt a sense of betrayal and emptiness. I figured that I had nothing to lose by allowing my father into my world. Meeting my father, at this point in my life, made me feel like I had just began reading a novel at the last chapter. Although my mother told us that Mr. Barnes had been a part of our lives when we were much younger, I did not remember. It was like meeting him for the very first time.

The food finally arrived at our table. After we enjoyed our meal, we proceeded to enter into Mr. Barnes' vehicle. Crossing the Verrazano Bridge relaxed me. I enjoyed the rippling waves of the ocean. The waves represented a sense of freedom for me. My life was new. I found the other part of me, my father.

Finally we arrived back in front of our project building. Mr. Barnes reached into his pocket and pulled out a fat roll of hundred dollar bills. He proceeded to give Dana three hundred dollars, and then he gave me three hundred dollars.

"Here," he stated, "go shopping and have a good time." Wow! I could not believe it! I never thought that I would see so much money!!

"Thank-you. This is for us?" I suspiciously questioned.

"Yes, call me later," he yelled, as he drove away from the brick building where we resided. Dana and I ran up the steps to our apartment. We were both in shock from all of the excitement, but we were very happy. As we entered into the apartment, we both held up the three hundred dollar bills that we had received from our father.

"Did you have fun?" questioned our mother, "and where did you get all of that money from?"

"Our father gave it to us. We're going shopping."

"Oh my goodness, why would your father give you so

much money? I mean, what are two kids supposed to do with all that money?" questioned my mother. "Oh, well, I guess he is making up for the past. You better get, while the getting is good," she abruptly stated, as she entered into her bedroom.

The next day Mr. Barnes called us in order to check up on us.

"How are you girls doing today?"

"We're good, but we don't have enough food in the house. My mother only has chicken in the freezer and we're hungry. Can you take us shopping?" Although our mother really had food in the house, we wanted Mr. Barnes to buy us most of the food that we saw on the television commercials.

"I'm really busy," replied Mr. Barnes, "but I can send somebody over there from Brooklyn with food." Dana and I gave him a list of all of the junk food and sweet cereals that we could handle.

After about two hours, a Cadillac pulled up in the front of our building, different from the Cadillac that our father drove. Dana and I were instructed to go downstairs with the shopping cart, in order to collect the food. The woman who got out of the vehicle appeared frightened. She was a fair-skinned woman in her early fifties. She was what I would classify as a little "chunky."

"Here's the food that you asked for," she stated as she rushed the food out of the trunk into our shopping cart. The woman sped off like she had just robbed a bank. Dana and I shouted "hooray" as we pushed the cart, overflowing with food, into the building.

We were so happy. We had money to spend, and had lots of food in the house. Dana and I decided to invite our friends Sheba, Veronica and Alice over for dinner. As they were approaching the apartment, Dana and I ran to the front door and unlocked it.

"Sheba, come here," I frantically screamed, "I met my father for the first time, and he gave us each three hundred dollars. Then we told him that we were hungry, and he sent somebody over here with a whole lot of food. Look," I stated as I opened the refrigerator that was stacked with food.

"Wow," stated Sheba, "you guys are really lucky."

"Yeah," I replied, "he's a very nice man. One day, very soon, you will meet him."

Many days passed by. Dana and I spoke to Mr. Barnes over the telephone. Springtime was just about to arrive. Dana and I needed new clothes. I decided to call Mr. Barnes and break the news to him.

"Hi, this is Sabrina."

"Sabrina, how are you and Dana?"

"Fine. Springtime is coming and I wanted to know if you would buy Dana and I some clothes."

"Oh, Sabrina," he reluctantly replied, "I won't have time. I mean, I'm so busy."

"I have the JC Penny's catalogue," I exclaimed. "Do you think that we could order some clothes and shoes from the catalogue? They are having a sale," I frantically shouted.

"There is no such thing as a sale," replied Mr. Barnes. "Well, okay, you and Dana order five hundred dollars worth of clothing each, and let me know when the order comes in.

"What, for real?" I replied.

"Yes," he replied, "I gotta go, see you," he stated as he abruptly hung up the phone.

Dana and I ordered trousers, sneakers, sandals, dresses, shirts and costume jewelry. The order finally came, and Mr. Barnes took us to JC Penny's in order to pick up the merchandise. When we got the boxes home, we ripped them open, and took out all of our clothes.

"Ooh, look what we got; I can't believe this," I exclaimed.

I went to school dressed to impress. My peers treated me much better, as a result of my dressing well. Everyone wanted to be my friend. Classmates came to our apartment for burgers, snacks, and fashion updates. Mr. Barnes called after two weeks and asked if we were okay.

"Sabrina, how would you like to go out to the Russian Tea Room for dinner? I will take you and a friend. After dinner we'll go see Jellie's Last Jam, which is a play. I will pick you up next Saturday. We'll have fun." I immediately hung up the phone and called Sheba.

"Sheba, my father said that I can invite a friend to go out to the Russian Tea Room Restaurant and then to a play. I want to take you, so that you can meet my father."

"Are you for real, Sabrina?" You know the Russian Tea Room is for millionaires. Who has money like that?"

"Trust me, Sheba, my father got it like that." We both laughed. "You just be ready and we will pick you up next Saturday at 2:00 p.m."

The days quickly rushed by. My father was on his way to pick me up, as usual, from in the front of the project building where I resided. I was dressed to impress. As I waited for my father, everyone passed by and stared. If was as if I were out of place, due to the dress code that I adopted for the occasion. Finally, Mr. Barnes pulled up in his 380 Mercedes.

"Get in, Sabrina," he stated as he stuck his head, full of grey hair, out the window of the vehicle. As usual, my father was dressed to kill. He had on a suede three piece suit, with suspenders. "You look nice, Sabrina," he stated as he kissed me on the cheek.

"This is one of the dresses that I ordered from the catalogue," I replied.

"It looks very nice on you, Sabrina, and I like your shoes. My shoes are Ballys'. . . I only wear Bally shoes," he boasted as he adjusted the speaker-phone system inside of his vehicle. "How do you like my new wheels?" he asked as he glanced into the side-view mirror. Although I had no idea what a Mercedes was, I pretended to know.

"Oh, wow, this is really nice," I replied.

"I am glad that you like the car, Sabrina. I paid fifty thousand dollars in cash for this car. I like to deal mostly with cash, although I am a millionaire in credit." I quickly changed the subject.

"I decided to bring my best friend, Sheba. I'll direct you to her building right over there," I stated as I pointed to the set of buildings behind the one where I resided. "She should be waiting in the front of her building." As we drove up to her building, Sheba walked up close to the vehicle. "Get in, girl," I exclaimed. "We're riding in style today." We both laughed. "Sheba, this is my father, Mr. Barnes."

"Hi, Mr. Barnes," Sheba replied in her Jamaican accent. "I have heard so much about you. It is nice to finally meet you. Sabrina told me that you were taking us to the Russian Tea Room. I apologize, but I didn't believe her. Nobody from these projects gets a chance to go to places like that."

"Are you kidding me?" replied Mr. Barnes, "I only go to the best places and give the best. *It is true*, we are going to that restaurant," he boasted.

"Wow," exclaimed Sheba. "That's what's up."

As we arrived at the valet parking lot, we were instructed to exit the vehicle. We walked up a flight of stairs into a large room which had high ceilings. Chandeliers hung above each table. The room was dimly lit, and I could smell the aroma of pastries. The large storm windows had beautiful burgundy satin curtains, which boldly hung down to the floor. Dimly lit candles were carefully placed in the center of each table. The room was cozy and beautiful. As we attempted to sit down in the chairs, two waiters, wearing white gloves, pulled out each chair and prompted us to sit. I could not believe what was actually happening. I could not describe the look on Sheba's face.

"So, young ladies, take a look at the menus and pick whatever you want." Wow, I was *really* starting to get used to all of this royal treatment. Was this for real? Was this all a dream? Sheba and I began to look at the menu. One entrée alone was at least one hundred fifty dollars. I looked at a "wine list," out of curiosity. I noticed a "Champagne List." The name that caught my eye was "Dom Pérignon" - $150.00. I thought that this was all a big joke. I would ask my father for a bottle of Dom Pérignon in order to share with Sheba. I've never had a drink, but it looked like fun, when I saw the celebrities on television do it. I had nothing to lose. Anyway, he was bound to say no.

"Hey, Mr. Barnes," I exclaimed, "I notice here – this bottle of champagne – one hundred fifty dollars; very expensive. Can Sheba and I order this?"

"Sabrina, I told you that you can order anything. Waiter," Mr. Barnes shouted, "give the young ladies a bottle of this," he stated as he pointed to the Dom Pérignon. What? I couldn't believe this. I was actually being treated like a queen. "Sabrina, I'm treating you how you should demand to be treated by men. You deserve the best, and it's my duty to demonstrate how you should be treated. You be sure to get your education, because that's the only way that you can compete. You have to be fit for your environment, in order to survive, or you will fall by the wayside," he exclaimed. "Oh, and don't take any wooden nickels." I felt as if my father were giving me a cram course in order to pass a final exam.

The champagne arrived and the waiter popped it open. "Ooh" exclaimed Sheba and I as the waiter poured the "bubbly" into the champagne glasses.

"I won't have any," stated Mr. Barnes, "I gave that up a long time ago." Sheba and I took a sip of champagne and chuckled. We were on top of the world. We ordered our meals and feasted like we were royal queens. Finally, dinner was over, and we arrived at the theatre. I did not want this night to ever end. After the entertainment was over, Mr. Barnes dropped Sheba and I off in the front of my building.

"Here you are," stated Mr. Barnes, as he handed Sheba and I five twenty dollar bills each. "Go out and have a good time, or better yet, buy yourselves something nice." Sheba's mouth dropped open.

"Thank you, sir," she responded. Although I was still in denial about all of the excitement, I could get used to this royal treatment.

Mr. Barnes called me one week later. "Sabrina, how did you and your friend Sheba enjoy the night on the town?" he asked.

"I had a wonderful time. Sheba really had fun, and she told me to thank you for showing her such a nice evening."

"The pleasure was all mine. I am glad that you both had fun," responded Mr. Barnes. "Like I said, that's how you should demand to be treated by a man. You don't have to date a man, just because he has a nice car, you can demand the whole package."

I began to feel as if my father was trying to make up for all of the years that he missed us growing up. Trying to play "catch-up" could be dangerous. Maybe he needed to over-compensate us, for his sake. I could play his game, for as long as he could last at playing it, or could I?

"Oh, summertime is coming, and Dana and I need summer clothes," I stated.

"Didn't you and Dana just order clothes? Okay, Sabrina,

you know what? I will take you and Dana shopping for summer clothes. You can bring along your friend, Sheba, and tell Dana to bring a friend." I was still in shock concerning all of this excitement.

Sheba, Dana, Veronica and I met Mr. Barnes in downtown Brooklyn. We all entered a store which had all name brand jeans, shoes, dresses, suits and slacks.

"Now all of you pick out whatever you want. We will go to the shoe department last," exclaimed Mr. Barnes.

We were actually on a *shopping spree*. I picked out five pairs of designer jeans, five suits, ten pairs of slacks and fifteen blouses. Once we all had picked out all of our merchandise, we put it on top of the counter next to the register.

"Are you all celebrating Christmas early?" questioned the cashier as she softly chuckled.

"No," replied Mr. Barnes, "I'm just treating them how they should be treated." While the cashier was ringing up the items, we all looked back and forth at each other in anticipation of hearing how much the bill would total.

After the cashier rang up the last item, she shouted, "The total amount for the order is $3,568.50." I looked around the room, attempting to avoid eye contact with my peers.

Mr. Barnes casually pulled out his credit card and stated, "I'll charge it, because I only have two thousand dollars cash on me."

After the clothing was paid for, we all grabbed our shopping bags. We had at least four shopping bags each. Before we exited the fifth floor, Mr. Barnes gave the cashier a forty dollar tip. We proceeded to the shoe department. We each picked out five pairs of shoes, one pair of Adidas, Pumas and Nikes. We stopped at the jewelry counters and were instructed by Mr. Barnes to pick out 14kt gold necklaces, bracelets and rings. We each picked out two bottles of expensive perfume. We had so many shopping bags. Mr. Barnes gave us each two hundred dollars, as we exited his vehicle, in order to go home. I still could not believe that we were being treated so well.

Mr. Barnes took us clothes shopping for every season that approached. We shopped for spring, summer, fall, and winter clothes. Dana and I had so many outfits that we literally had to walk on the top of our clothes in order to get to the other side of our room. Some clothes that were on the floor still had price tags on them. We had leather coats, blazers, sheepskin coats, and every item of fashion that was popular, thanks to Mr. Barnes. He also bought Dana and I big boxes of chocolate on every Valentine's Day. We each had a "boom box," which played the latest hits of the eighties. Mr. Barnes even refurnished our entire apartment, after we complained about how embarrassed we were to have company, due to the outdated condition of the apartment. Mr. Barnes ordered a glass table for the kitchen that accompanied four green velour chairs. All of the rooms were garnished with wall-to-wall plush carpeting. Mr. Barnes bought two twin canopy bedroom sets for the room that Dana and I shared. Dana and I each had our own color television, VCR, and boom-box in the room. People began to call us "poor little rich girls." Aunt Carey and her kids began to hate us even more because of the way that Mr. Barnes treated us.

Although Mr. Barnes' shopping sprees began to decrease, he still found a way to do what I called a "drive-by." Mr. Barnes would tell me to meet him downstairs, and he would hand me hundreds of dollars and quickly leave. I began to feel abandoned and empty, although the material goods were abundant. I began to feel out of place. The moment that I walked out of my apartment, reality hit me. I was really a poor little rich girl, still consumed by the hands of the projects. My mind began to grow weary, as a result of the camouflages that Mr. Barnes was painting into the forefront of my mind. I wanted a relationship with my father. I wanted to get to know who he was. I began to get tired of money, clothes and jewelry being thrown at me. I decided to let Mr. Barnes know how I was feeling about our father/daughter relationship. I dialed Mr. Barnes' number hoping that he was available.

"Hello, barber shop."

"Hi, may I speak to Mr. Barnes? This is his daughter, Sabrina." While waiting for my father to come to the telephone I heard him yell.

"He better give me back my money, it is the principle, I have had many legs broken." After waiting for about three minutes, Mr. Barnes came to the phone.

"Hello?"

"Hi, this is Sabrina."

"Can you kind of make it quick? I'm really very busy," stated Mr. Barnes.

"Mr. Barnes, I just wanted to say that I appreciate all that you do for me. I mean, my life has drastically changed since we've met. I would really like to spend some quality time with you. I am your daughter, but I just don't feel like I really know you. Do you think that we could go on vacation as a family, or maybe I could make dinner for you, over here?"

"Thanks, Sabrina, I would love to do all of those things with you, but I'm very busy here at the barber shop. You like nice things, don't you?"

"Yes," I replied.

"Well, I will let you know when you could come over to Brooklyn in order to pick up some money from me here at the barber shop. Make sure you call me first, okay, don't just show up."

I thought that it would be a nice surprise if I showed up at the barber shop in Brooklyn. Mr. Barnes would be happy to see me. I arrived in the front of the barber shop, one of the buildings that my father owned. There was a man standing in the front of the building wearing an umpire's mask on his face. I thought that this was strange, but I proceeded to enter into the barber shop anyway. As I entered through the door, a man stopped me.

"May I help you?" he asked.

"I'm here to see Mr. Barnes; he's my father," I cheerfully replied.

"Oh, wait right here." Before I could respond, Mr. Barnes ran towards me and began screaming.

"I told you not to come here without calling. Are you crazy? Do you want someone to kidnap you? Come here," he stated as he grabbed my hand, and walked me towards the back of the barber shop. All of a sudden I felt as if I were in Atlantic City. There were slots, other gaming machines and people running frantically back and forth shouting out numbers. "Sabrina, this is a numbers hole. I own this," he stated as a detective walked by and accepted cash from Mr. Barnes. "I don't want you around here. It could be dangerous." Mr. Barnes was dressed in his usual three-piece suit, suspenders and dress shoes. Everyone in his presence appeared to be subdued by his demeanor. "Come on, Sabrina, I'll take you up the street. You can sit with a friend of mine. Her name is Mrs. Brenda Smythe. She owns a balloon shop. I'm going to be too busy to keep you company for now. In the meantime, take this five hundred dollars. You can go shopping after you sit with Mrs. Smythe for a while. You can take the Mercedes."

While we walked up the street, Mr. Barnes handed me the keys to his vehicle. "Sabrina, don't take anything from this woman," he demanded. "If she gives you anything or offers a service, don't accept." We walked into a storefront where the windows were covered with balloons and stuffed animals. As we entered the store, I could smell the aroma of incense, perfume, and flowers. A woman came out from the back of the store. She was a dark-complexioned woman with long black hair. She wore a long red dress, and had eyes like flames of fire. As she came closer to us, the flames in her eyes diminished. There was something completely mystical about this woman.

"Hi, Mrs. Smythe."

"Oh, hi, Mr. Barnes. How are you today?"

"This is my daughter, Sabrina."

"Nice to meet you," I reluctantly replied.

"Sabrina is going to sit with you for a while and then she's going shopping. I just don't want her around the barber shop, if you know what I mean."

"Yes, sir, I know what you mean," she replied. "I'll watch over her, don't you worry about a thing." Mr. Barnes hastily walked out of the store.

"So, Sabrina," stated Mrs. Smythe, "have a seat. Where do you live?"

"Oh, I'm from Staten Island."

"Do you like it over there?" she cunningly asked.

"It's okay, I guess, for the time being."

"Sabrina, do you know anything about baths?"

"You mean bubble baths?" I innocently questioned.

"No, I mean spiritual baths. I can see *things* around you. It's not good. I could give you a bath that would change things for the better, for your life now, and in the future. It would only cost you five hundred dollars."

"What, for a bath?" I shouted. "I don't have that kind of money."

"Well, Sabrina, you father has so much money, you should

ask him for it because you need this bath. If you don't do it, the curse is going to follow you. It may not hurt you now, but in the future, it will find you." At this point I was more than afraid. My father had told me not to take anything from her. I didn't. It was given to me –the possibility of having a curse attack me in the future. I began to panic.

"Okay, Mrs. Smythe, I will ask him." Mrs. Smythe began to show me around the shop.

"This is the tub that I will bathe you in," she stated as she pointed to a small white tub located in the middle of the hallway. Mrs. Smythe began to show me a deck of cards which had strange symbols written on them. Before she was able to explain what the cards represented, Mr. Barnes hastily entered back into Mrs. Smythe's store.

"Oh, Sabrina, I almost forgot." When Mr. Barnes saw Mrs. Smythe showing me the mystical deck of cards, he became hysterical. "Sabrina, didn't I tell you not to accept anything from her? What are you doing?"

"I'm not doing anything. She was just telling me about a bath or something," I innocently replied.

"Sabrina, I think that you should be leaving. You have quite a bit of shopping to do," Mr. Barnes stated as he pulled me by the arm out of Mrs. Smythe's "Balloon Shop."

I began to feel confused. I was confused about the way that Mr. Barnes treated me. I was confused concerning who or what he actually represented, and how his presence would affect my life. The beginning of my life was just about to start. I would move forward with Mr. Barnes' affection or without his affection . . .

PART II

It was the year 1989. I was a sophomore, attending Wagner College. I was very happy at the time because within two more years I would be graduating from college. I was also elated because I had a wardrobe that everyone admired, and I was the perfect role model in college. Writing papers all day, quoting Shakespeare and visiting the library were starting to bore me. On one cold winter day I decided to take a break from my studies and go for a ride on the Staten Island Ferry. As I sat down on my seat, I noticed a young man seated across from me. He was quite attractive, tall and had a distinctive gleam in his eyes. He was accompanied by a little boy and girl. I felt the urge to speak to him. Finally, I got up enough courage and spoke to the young man.

"Hello," my name is Sabrina.

"Hi," he said, "my name is Keno. Are you from Brooklyn?"

"No," I replied, "I'm a Staten Island girl." We both chuckled. He proceeded to introduce the little boy.

"This is my younger brother. His name is Johnny. He is nine years old. This is my sister, Sandra. She is seven years old."

The two youngsters appeared quite friendly. We exchanged numbers and I promised Keno that I would call him. A week after I called Keno. On that particular day, Keno invited me out to dinner. At first I was ashamed to give him my address, because I lived in the Stapleton Projects. Stapleton was one of the primary ghettos of Staten Island. This was a place where many individuals had to literally fight in order to survive. This was a place where you either allow the beast to rule you, or you found enough courage to establish a game of survival. I figured that I had nothing to lose. I finally gave Keno my address.

"Fine," stated Keno, "I will pick you up on Friday at 8:00 p.m."

I was so excited. On Friday night, Keno picked me up for our dinner date. I could not help but notice the same gleam that appeared in his eyes when I first met him.

"Hi," exclaimed Keno as I sat down in the vehicle.

I replied, "Hello."

This was, in fact, the first time that I actually went on a genuine date. As we drove down the streets of Staten Island, I could not help but notice the neighborhoods that we passed. There were all beautiful homes with manicured lawns, scenery that I was generally quite unfamiliar with.

"So how long have you been living on Staten Island?" asked Keno.

"I actually grew up on Staten Island," I cheerfully replied.

"Interesting, Sabrina," Keno replied. "I have been living on Staten Island for five years. I'm originally from New Jersey. I live in my parents' home, in the Mariners Harbor section of the island. I am a part time college student, and I work full time for a New York City agency."

As he finished his sentence, we pulled up into the driveway of a well-known restaurant. "WINDOWS ON WONDERS" read the awning above the restaurant. As I looked up, I could not help but notice the tapered-glossy windows of the restaurant, along with the gleaming lights, which appeared magical. We entered into the restaurant and there were freshly picked flowers, and a dimly-lit candle on each table. The entire room was also lit dimly. I noticed the reflection of the candle lights move slowly across Keno's handsome face. I could feel my mind literally racing, hoping that the evening would turn out perfect.

As the waiter sat us at the table, I asked Keno to excuse me while I went to the ladies' room. When I entered the ladies' room I noticed a mirror on the wall encircled by the brightest bubble lights that I have ever seen! As I looked into the mirror and saw the bright reflection of my face, I heard a familiar voice of a female speak to me. She said, "Be yourself. If you are yourself, he will get to know you. If you pretend to be someone else, he will not get to know you. Relax and let the evening flow naturally." As I looked away from the mirror, I felt a strong urgency to return back to the table in order to accompany Keno.

When I arrived back at the table the waiter had already placed two glasses of iced water and a basket of hot bread in the center of the table. Keno and I ordered our food. We were enjoying each other's conversation during the meal. At the end of the evening, Keno dropped me off in the front of my building. "181 GORDON STREET" read the bold-lettered sign on the front of the project building where I resided. As I opened the car door in order to get out, I noticed about fifteen men who appeared to be in their mid-twenties jogging in line. They appeared quite disciplined. The men resembled soldiers training for war. They all had serious looks on their faces and had bodies of steel. This was not the first time that I'd seen these young men around the neighborhood. I was informed in the past that they were the famous Paris Crew who lived in the Stapleton Projects where I resided. Although I had heard about all of the other neighborhoods that they had conquered, I was not afraid. They never bothered me.

"Good night," stated Keno.

"Good night," I replied.

"I will call you tomorrow," exclaimed Keno.

I shut the door to Keno's vehicle and watched him fade away into the evening sunset.

Eight months had already passed by, and Keno and I were getting to know each other by spending a lot of quality time together, talking, going to the movies, and enjoying intimate times together. As far as I was concerned, Keno was my king. There was nothing that I would not do in order to keep him by my side. I started to feel like Keno was all that I had, ever had, and ever would have. I felt as if I were mysteriously falling in love with Keno. I always looked forward to spending time with him.

It was a bright sunny day when I visited Keno at his parents' home. I could feel the warm, hot sun beaming down on my freshly-crimped hair. I could smell the illuminating smell of newly-lit charcoal in the air. The children on Keno's block were cheerfully playing in the middle of the street. As I entered Keno's residence, Keno's mother, Ms. Williams, was in the kitchen preparing a meal.

"Hello, Sabrina."

"Hello," I exclaimed in a soft monotone voice.

She was a fair-skinned woman in her mid-forties, with locks in her hair. She seemed quite happy with her profession as a registered nurse. I sat in the chair while Ms. Williams was seasoning her stew while standing. Well, I had known Ms. Williams for at least eight months now. She had been divorced from Mr. Williams for three years. I have never seen her in the company of a man since I had been visiting. I often saw a particular female visit Ms. Williams. She seemed a little older than Ms. Williams.

"Well, you and Keno seem to be getting along just fine, Sabrina."

"Yes," I replied, "Keno makes me very happy and I finally feel like my life is completed."

"That is very good," replied Ms. Williams. "Oh, by the way, Sabrina, if you don't mind, I will need you to baby-sit little John and Sandra, maybe every evening from now on, until further notice."

Well, Ms. Williams was a bold soul with words.

"I may need you to cook for them, make sure that their hair is combed and make sure that they are ready for school the next day. Perhaps you may need to move in."

"Well," I replied, "that doesn't seem like a bad idea. It beats staying home, living in a cramped room without Keno."

"I have already discussed the situation with Keno, and he was fine with the idea."

"Fine," I replied. Besides, my classes were in the morning. "I will gather my belongings together and have Keno bring them over."

Abruptly, Ms. Williams leaned over and whispered in my ear, "I must confess, Sabrina, the female that you see visiting me often. That is my lover. Her name is Rosa. I am gay."

Before I was able to respond, I noticed that Keno had been in the living room listening to our conversation.

"Oh, my goodness," Keno exclaimed, "my mother is gay."

Keno proceeded to run up the stairs. Ms. Williams and I proceeded to run after him. Keno slammed his bedroom door.

"I need to speak to Sabrina alone. Mom, do not come in here," he yelled as he stood behind the locked bedroom door. Finally, Ms. Williams hastily walked downstairs, and Keno opened the door with his eyes bloodshot red, filled with tears.

"I am sorry," I exclaimed. I was brought up in a Christian home where we were taught that men should be with women, and women with men. Either way, I would not discriminate. I am not one to judge. People do what they do.

"I never knew that my mother was gay," exclaimed Keno. "She never told me. Why? How could she do this?"

"Well, Keno, that is a question that you will need to ask your mother. I am certain that your mother did not intend to hurt you. Everything will be fine, Keno," I stated as I hugged Keno and wiped the tears from his bloodshot eyes. "Remember, Keno, I am here for you. It will be okay."

"Thank you," replied Keno. "Later on I will drive you to your home so that you can pick up your belongings."

"Fine," I replied as I walked downstairs into the cold, dreary living room. I thought to myself, "How am I going to tell my mother that I'm moving out, into Keno's home?" My mother was a very old fashioned Christian woman. I wondered how I was going to convince her that this would be the best decision for me.

Keno had just returned from the corner store. "Okay, Sabrina, I am ready to drive you to your mother's home so that you can pick up your clothing." As we were driving along the ritzy neighborhoods of the island, Keno was staring blankly into the rear view mirror of the car. For some strange reason the ride to my mother's house seemed longer than usual.

"Bye, Keno," I stated as I opened the car door of his vehicle.

"I will meet you later, at my mother's house," replied Keno.

I hastily ran to my building, got into the elevator, and pressed the #7 button. When the elevator door opened, I ran to apartment 7C and knocked on the front door. My mother opened the door with a shrewd smile on her face.

"Hello, Sabrina. How are you today?"

"Fine, Mom. I need to talk to you about Keno. His mother told me that she is gay. Keno overheard her telling me, and he is very upset about the situation. He did not take it too well," I exclaimed. I could not get up enough courage to tell my mother that I was moving out, into Keno's house. After all, my mother was no fool.

"Mom, I need to stay over Keno's house for a few days out of the week. I am not actually moving in, but I will be assisting Ms. Williams with the kids until she settles a situation that she is dealing with at this time."

"Sabrina, you know how I feel about one spending nights with a mate before marriage, but if you believe that this is the right decision for your life, you are free to go."

Wow! I was expecting my mother to hit the roof, especially since she had met Keno in person only five times with the past five months. She always spoke kindly to him over the telephone when he called in order to speak to me, and vice versa. Perhaps my mother finally realized that I was getting older. Besides, she had my sister who is two years younger than me. She always kept my mother company. My father had never lived with us, so my mother must have subconsciously accepted my quest for a dominant father figure in my life. I began to calmly pack some of my clothing into a suitcase.

Over time, staying at Keno's house for a few days out of the week turned into weeks at a time. I found myself struggling to stay on top of my studies. I was beginning to feel like the live-in maid. I was cooking, shopping, and cleaning for Keno and his younger siblings, while Ms. Williams disappeared on her rendezvous with her lover, Rosa.

It had been three months since I had been living with Keno and his family. One cold morning when I woke up, the house seemed very dreary and cold. I glanced at the clock, and it read 6:00 a.m. I got out of the bed and looked for Keno, but he was no place to be found. I walked downstairs into the kitchen, then into the living room, and nobody was there. I found that to be quite unusual, since someone was always at home during the morning. I looked into John and Sandra's room and it was empty. I looked into Ms. Williams' room, and it was also empty. I proceeded to go back upstairs into Keno's room—the room that we shared. As I opened the door to the bathroom, an automatic light switched on, and on the mirror was written in red lipstick—SABRINA WILL YOU MARRY ME? An arrow was pointed downward. I proceeded to move slowly, closer towards the sink. Inside the sink, under the pointed arrow, was a box. I abruptly opened the box, and there it was—a beautiful diamond engagement ring. It was the most beautiful diamond that I had ever seen!! I screamed in a loud voice, and began to cry.

I began to exclaim, "Yes, Keno, I will marry you."

I immediately put the ring onto my finger, vowing never to take it off. I hastily ran into the bedroom and called my mother. I was so excited!!

"Hello," exclaimed my mother.

"Hi, Mom, this is Sabrina," I stated breathlessly. "Keno just proposed to me. He left the ring in a box inside of the sink. He wrote in red lipstick on the mirror, "Would you marry me?" I was talking so fast that I could hardly speak clearly.

"Oh, dear daughter, congratulations," exclaimed my mother. "I'm very happy for the both of you. I really hope that everything works out well for the both of you."

"Thanks, Mom. I am so happy."

"Well, Sabrina, where is Keno?"

"When I woke up early this morning, he was not here. Actually, Mom, nobody was home at all. I am so excited about the plans that I have to make regarding our wedding. Don't you remember, Mom, that peach and grey are my favorite colors? Those are the colors that I am going to pick for the wedding. As soon as Keno and I pick a wedding date, I will inform the rest of the family regarding our engagement. Tell my sister Dana the good news. I am certain that she will be excited." Well, my sister Dana was not very fond of Keno. She just tolerated him because I tolerated her friends. I guess that the old saying is true. One hand washes the other and they both wash your face.

"Okay, Sabrina," replied my mother. "I will speak to you later. You two be good to each other."

"Okay, goodbye," I said. I immediately rushed back into the bathroom and took a nice, warm shower. I must have been in the shower for at least twenty minutes or so. When I got out of the shower, Keno was sitting on the bed, dressed in a white tuxedo, holding a bouquet of roses. I abruptly ran over to him, wrapped in my towel, and said, "Yes, I will marry you."

"I love you Sabrina," stated Keno.

I replied, "I love you too."

Keno began to softly kiss my lips. Keno abruptly interrupted our intimate moment when he exclaimed, "Sabrina, get dressed." Keno slowly opened the closet. There it was— the most beautiful peach-colored satin gown that I have ever seen!!!

Keno said, "Sabrina, try it on." The gown was satin-peach with white roses around the waist. The thin white straps casually hung off my shoulders. There was a sexy slit that accented the left side of my thigh. I was dressed to kill. I fixed my hair in a French roll, put on my black patent leather pumps, and we were ready to go.

"Oh, Keno, by the way—where are we going?" I asked with a shrewd smile.

"Just step outside, my sweetheart Sabrina, and you will see for yourself." As I slowly opened the front door of the house, I noticed that there was a white stretched limousine parked in the driveway.

"Oh, no, you didn't," I shouted in a loud monotone voice.

"Yes, I did," shouted Keno.

"Come on, Keno, let's go." We hastily got into the ritzy limousine. The old-fashioned digital clock read 11:30 a.m. There were two bottles of Moet champagne chilling over a bucket of ice.

"Oh, Keno, this is so romantic!! This is so beautiful. I do not know what else to say. You made me so happy. I want to spend the rest of my life with you."

"You are very special to me, Sabrina. I don't ever want to lose you. I love you, baby girl."

Keno and I had lunch at a beautiful restaurant by the seaside. We spent hours riding around town in the limousine drinking champagne and listening to music.

"This has been a day to remember," stated Keno. The clock in the limousine read 6 o'clock p.m. It was time to go home. The limousine driver dropped us off at home. The day was over. The memories would always be unforgettable.

Today was my day!! I called my best friend Sheba and gave her the good news. "Hello, Sheba, this is Sabrina."

"Hi, Sabrina."

"I am calling you in order to tell you that Keno and I have gotten engaged. We don't have a wedding date set at this time, but I'd just like to prepare you. I am asking you to be my maiden of honor."

"Fantastic," replied Sheba. "It would be an honor to accept that position. Congratulations."

"Thank you," I replied. "Just imagine, Sheba, everyone will be calling me Mrs. Williams."

We both chuckled.

"Yeah, girl. No more single life."

"I want our wedding colors to be peach and grey," I told Sheba.

"So, how many people are going to be at the wedding?" asked Sheba.

"Oh, about one hundred fifty," I replied. "You know, Keno's family is really big."

"I know what you mean," stated Sheba. "Oh, Sabrina, I know that you are going to have the deejay at the reception play that song 'Whip Appeal.' You know, that song by Babyface that you and Keno always listen to."

"Girl, I am going to be on cloud nine on the wedding day. Between the cake, the pictures, the wedding party, and everything else that I'm going to be doing, I probably will not have time to remember to tell the DJ to play that song."

"Yeah, Sabrina, that day is going to be a very exciting day for the both of you."

"Okay, Sheba, I will call you later on. Goodnight."

I abruptly hung up the telephone. I prepared my bubble bath and relaxed. I played our song by Babyface, "Whip Appeal," as I sat in the warm bubble bath. "Whatever you want, it's alright with me, 'cause you got that whip appeal . . ."

The next morning, I woke up with a new outlook on life. I opened up my bedroom window. I could feel the cool breeze move across my face. I was special. I felt different. I finally felt like my life had been defined. The telephone rang. It was Keno. He was on his lunch hour. For some strange reason, the phone rang louder than usual.

41

"Hello," I stated as I answered the telephone.

"Hello, Sabrina," stated Keno, "I need to talk with you."

"About what?" I replied. I was so nervous about the way that he approached me, but I could not dare give him any clue that I was in any way concerned.

"You know, Sabrina, I love you so much that I am going to pick out a more expensive engagement ring for you, but before I do so, I need to sit down with you in person and go over a few things with you." Well, Keno for the most part was a very straight-forward young man with his words.

"Okay, Keno, I will call you when I finish my classes tomorrow. Also, I am spending the night at my mother's home."

"Fine," replied Keno.

All the while I was wondering, what could Keno want to talk to me about? Why would he want to replace the ring that he gave me? After all, Keno was all that I had, at least in my mind. I was desperate to find out what Keno wanted to talk to me about. I would do anything to keep him in my life.

It was a hot morning when Keno drove up to the school campus that I attended, in order to meet me for lunch. I had finished my classes for the day. When Keno arrived, I could smell the distinguished aroma of his cologne. His eyes appeared to have the same gleam that they had when we first met.

"Hello, Sabrina."

"Hello, Keno," I replied with a subtle tremor in my voice, as I sat in the vehicle. This was the first time in my life that I actually felt like I was in love. I grew up in a single-parent home. My mother was alone, raising the two of us without my father, Mr. Barnes, as they called him. Mr. Barnes was a married man who had two children from a previous marriage. He also had a mistress who had a biological 19-year old son with him. She was also married. I always wondered why my mother had the two of us with a married man. Even though it was not correct in the eyes of God, I was glad to be part of the land of the living. Besides, my mother had been delivered from her past. Although he was not living with us, I still loved him. He was a "book smart" and a "street smart" man. I knew not to compare Keno with my father. Since meeting Keno, I had been spending less time with my father. I vowed to wait until the wedding plans were made before "spilling the beans" about Keno and I being engaged. My father always appreciated the finished product, no matter what it was. During most of our conservations, I always kept dear old dad in the back of my mind.

The place where Keno and I were dining for lunch was what I considered sort of "shabby." "RIB SHACK" read the bold red letters on the front of the glass window. The withered menu taped to the splinter-surfaced wood door read "lunch special." I could not dare let Keno know how nervous I was about this meeting. My facial expression could not hide the way that I was feeling.

"Sabrina, let us get a table for two," exclaimed Keno.

"Fine," I replied.

"Waiter," shouted Keno, "we would like a booth, two for lunch." As the waiter escorted us to the booth by the window, I noticed the freshly picked flowers placed in the center of the table. As we sat at the table, it began to get very cloudy, and shortly it began to rain. "Pitter-patter, pitter-patter," I heard as the large raindrops hit the window pane. The rain drops seemed as though they were getting louder and louder.

The waiter asked, "May I get you something to drink?"

"Yes," Keno replied, "I will have a glass of lemonade."

"I will have a glass of iced tea," I stated as I glanced at the large raindrops on the window pane. As the waiter walked

43

away, I stared Keno in the eyes. For some strange reason, his pupils were much larger than usual.

"Sabrina, I have been thinking. You already know that I am working full time during the day, and going to school part-time in the evening. I respect the fact that you are in college full-time. You know, Sabrina, I am in need of a little help from you financially. You know, I just believe that we should be doing the same things. I think that you should get a full time job and transfer from Wagner College into a City University school. You could take your classes part-time until you obtain your degree. Just imagine, Sabrina, we could save some money and get our own apartment."

Well, I was so shocked. I could not believe what Keno was saying to me. I did not understand where this request came from. It seemed as if it came out of the raindrops that were continuously hitting the window pane. Why would Keno ask me to transfer from the private school that I was attending, especially since I was at the end of my junior year in college? Besides, I worked so hard to get into the school that I attend, and it is a private school. Many people would be very thankful to be in my shoes. Not to mention the scholarships and the grants that I was given towards my tuition. Although I was very disturbed about his request, I pretended to be elated.

"Keno, that would be a great idea! Besides, we could plan our wedding in privacy, in our own apartment."

"Sabrina, I am so happy that you are in agreement with my vision concerning our future."

As Keno finished his sentence, the waiter asked, "What will you be ordering today?" Although all of a sudden I was in no mood to eat, I abruptly responded, "I will have a cheese-burger and fries with a fruit punch, please."

Keno stated, "I will have the same." As the waiter picked up the menus and walked away, Keno looked into my eyes and said, "Sabrina, this is great!!" We sat in silence for about fifteen minutes. I could sense Keno's mind racing to and fro. Finally, Keno decided to break the silence.

"You know, Sabrina, I think that I would have a good chance of getting you a job with the agency that I work with. As a matter of fact, there is a clerical position downtown that is available. The starting salary is eighteen thousand dollars a year. If we add up the twenty-five thousand dollars a year that I make, we would have forty-three thousand dollars a year in total. We would be able to get a nice apartment, save some money and be independent," Keno stated as the waiter placed our meal in front of us. "I have a great rapport with upper-management within the agency that I work for. With your skills, and my reputation, you would have no problem getting hired, in no time. You know, Sabrina, I could even get you an interview, as soon as next week. The director of the department, Mr. Greenstein, is a very nice man. How's that sound?" Well, Keno was pretty charming with his words. I couldn't dare disappoint him by dismissing his proposal.

"Alright," I said, as I put a greasy French fry into my mouth.

Keno replied, "I will contact Mr. Greenstein next week in order to schedule the interview."

"That sounds great." While Keno was driving me to my mother's house, I suddenly felt as if my entire world with Keno was slowly collapsing.

"Oh, Sabrina," Keno exclaimed as he glanced at my butter-creamed complexion face. "Don't forget to bring the rest of your clothes from your mom's house next week when you come over since you will be moving permanently into my mother's home with me, until we get our new apartment." As Keno drove away, I could feel the sudden discomfort of my mind struggling with my emotions regarding the situation.

A week had quickly passed by. I was on my way to Keno's mother's house—permanently. It was a bright sunny day. As I approached the front door of Keno's mother's house, holding my suitcase, I noticed the numbers on the battered heavy wooden door which read, 455 South Avenue. The numbers on the house appeared much larger than usual for some strange reason. Before I was able to ring the bell, Ms. Williams abruptly opened the door. She obviously had been watching me approach the front gate, from the window upstairs.

"Hello, Sabrina."

"Hello, Ms. Williams."

"So," stated Ms. Williams, as she glanced at me from the side of her almond-shaped eye, "Keno tells me that you will be starting a full time job with the City. That is so nice. You know, consider yourself lucky that you pulled that one off so fast," she stated as she clapped her hands together. "So, is it true that you are going to transfer to a City school? "You may lose some credits, and how many people from the Stapleton projects where you grew up actually get a chance to step foot into Wagner College?"

Well, Ms. Williams must have been reading my mind. Although I agreed with her regarding her notion, I would not dare tell her. I was determined to play along with their game, as long as I could get away with it.

"So," stated Ms. Williams, "once you start your new job, you and Keno could save some money so that you can get an apartment together, and plan a life for yourselves. How lovely," stated Ms. Williams as she glanced out of the front window, pretending to be preoccupied with something or someone outside. Ms. Williams was really starting to irritate me with her phony best wishes. I never really felt as if Ms. Williams genuinely appreciated my kindness or presence. I always felt as if she always pretended that she liked me. I guess that we both just tolerated each other for Keno's sake.

"Well," I softly stated, "I have not confirmed a definite date with Keno, regarding transferring schools, or accepting a full-time position." Ms. Williams appeared to have no problem with jumping to conclusions.

"Well," stated Ms. Williams, "Keno is upstairs. By the way, Sabrina, I am going out with Rosa this weekend. I will need you to cook for John and Sandra; oh, and you know the routine, please make sure that their hair is combed." I could slowly feel the mark "SLAVE" being branded on my forehead and "MOLLY MAID" branded on my chest. As I proceeded up the stairs, I could hear Keno speaking on the telephone.

"Yeah, Marky," Keno loudly shouted, "I think that it would be a great idea. Okay, we'll see you tomorrow." As Keno was putting down the telephone, I entered the bedroom.

"Hey, what's up, Sabrina, how was your day?"

"My day was fine," I stated as Keno plopped a quick, wet kiss on my lips.

Before I could even utter another word, Keno exclaimed, "I was just speaking with my old buddy, Marky. You know, the guy that you saw me with at the club back in the day," he said as he softly chucked. "You might have heard me talking about him. He is also engaged. He and his fiancee will be in town for about two months. I thought that it would be a great idea if all four of us went out in order to celebrate." Keno always had a way of dictating plans before confirming them with me. "Sabrina, we have arranged to meet tomorrow evening, at the Placid Restaurant, across the street from the Underground Club in Manhattan."

As Keno finished speaking, I *slowly* began to remember his old buddy Marky from the past. It was a gloomy Saturday, about four months ago, when I visited Keno. In my mind, I was really looking forward to spending the entire evening with him, alone. As I walked up to the front entrance and rang the bell, I could hear Keno's favorite "house music" playing very loudly. "Break for Love" was the song playing. Keno loved to dance, and I could feel his energy pierce through my chest from the front entrance. I hastily rang the bell again. Evidently, there was nobody home with Keno. He was obviously unable to hear the bell, because the music was too loud. I turned the doorknob, and to my surprise, the door was open. I proceeded to walk up the creaky-sounding steps into Keno's room. As I entered the room, I saw Keno dancing to his house music, as he was getting dressed. Well, I thought, it's only four o'clock in the afternoon. If I were one to go to clubs, it would be definitely too early for me to be partying.

"Keno, what's up with all of that loud music, and why are you all dressed up?" Keno had on a pair of neatly pressed black dress slacks, a silk, white turtle-neck shirt, and a multi-colored vest. My man was in style. He had on the latest floor-shine shoes that the average "pretty boy" would kill for. Keno sported the fade haircut, which was very popular among the young men of the eighties. The style really looked good on him.

"Sabrina, I know that I promised that we'd go to a movie tonight, but Marky called me and I have portrayed tonight as 'boys' night out.'"

Well, I was appalled. The least he could have done was called me at my mother's house in order to save me a trip over here, only to discover that my evening had been ruined. Who was I fooling? Any other time, I would stay home and wait for Keno to return from his escapades. I was determined that on this night, no matter what, Sabrina would not stay home and wait for him.

"So, what time are you and Marky meeting?"

"Oh," Keno replied, "I'd say that I should be leaving here

at about five o'clock so that I could pick him up from his Aunt Betty's house in Bayonne, New Jersey."

Well, Keno drove a 1988 two-door, light-blue Nissan Maxima. He was pretty good at maneuvering his faithful stick shift vehicle.

"So, Keno, where are you and Marky going to hang out at?" I asked with a phony smile.

"Oh, we're going to meet a couple of the fellas at the good old Underground Club in Manhattan. You know, just to chill out and catch up on the latest dance moves."

I trusted Keno, but I didn't trust myself. I was a quite attractive female, but Keno, he had a face that the females lived for. We would ride on the bus together at times, and I would literally catch other females giving him the complete stare-down.

"Yeah, I know what you mean," I said abruptly. "It's been a while since I spent time with my best friend, Sheba. I know what you mean."

Before I knew it, the grandfather clock struck five o'clock p.m. Keno was doing the finishing touches on his outfit.

"Well, Sabrina, I will see you when I get back."

Whenever Keno went out on "boy's night," I never saw him until the next morning. I was determined that it would not happen. No, not on this boys' night out. I would not sit up and wait for him to come home.

"Okay, Keno, have a nice time," I stated after he gave me a quick kiss on my gold colored painted lips. I hastily followed him downstairs and locked the door behind him. As I walked back up the stairs, I could hear Keno start the motor of his car. When I entered the bedroom, I looked out of the window into the dreary driveway. Keno was backing the vehicle out into the street. Finally, he was clear out of the driveway, on the way to his destination. I immediately ran back downstairs into the kitchen and picked up the telephone. I dialed my best friend Sheba's number as fast as I could. "Ring, ring," the phone rang at least five times. As I listened to the number of telephone rings increase, I could feel the sigh of desperation consuming my mind. I was hoping that Sheba was at home. Finally, the answering machine picked up. "Hi, I can't come to the phone, but please leave a message." I began leaving a message when Sheba abruptly interrupted the answering machine.

"Hello," exclaimed Sheba with a raspy Jamaican accent.

"Thank God," I shouted. "Sheba, this is Sabrina."

"Hey girl, what's up?" replied Sheba.

"I need your help," I demanded.

"What is it?"

"Keno and his friends are going out to the Underground Club. You know, the reggae club over in Manhattan."

"Yeah, but since when does Keno like reggae?"

"He really doesn't but on Friday nights the club has a house music marathon, or something. Anyway, I wanted to know if you would come with me to the club so that I could spy on him. I mean, I trust him but I just want to make sure that he has no hidden agendas when it comes to other females. I don't know, but sometimes I feel like there is somebody else. I guess it's just the club 'thing' that I'm uncomfortable with."

Well, Sheba was a hard-core Jamaican yardee. She was born in Jamaica, West Indies, but she came to this country when she was about eight years old. She left the island of Jamaica, but the island never left her. Sheba loved reggae music. She would not dare refuse to accompany me to the reggae club. I have known Sheba for at least ten years. She practically grew up with me in the Stapleton Projects. I knew most of her family who lived in the States at the time and she knew my family, including my father, Mr. Barnes. Basically, I trusted her.

"You want to spy, Sabrina?" questioned Sheba with an undertone of motherly love.

"Yeah, spy," I abruptly responded. "I do not think that it is too bad of an idea. I mean—what is the worst thing that could happen? I could bust him on a date with a female that I probably know." I could feel my imagination running wildly, into information that was not even valid until Sheba abruptly interrupted me.

"Sabrina, I will go with you to the club; however, don't blame me if you catch him out on a date with one of our male math teachers from junior high school." We both chuckled.

"Thanks, Sheba, you're the greatest. I am going down to the car rental shop. I will call you once I get the vehicle in my possession. I already know the directions to the club. I mean, it's not that far, after all. Sheba, start getting dressed for the occasion, and be certain that you are dressed to impress."

"Okay," Sheba excitedly responded. "I will wait for your call."

As I hung up the telephone, I could feel a big chill of revenge run up my spine. I planned to be the best dressed female in the club tonight. I was convinced that there would be nobody else to compete with me for my man. I abruptly ran upstairs and opened the closet door. I picked across two dresses, one blue, one black. Nah, I was feeling in the mood to wear red.

I quickly pushed back the two hangers and BAM, there it was—my beautiful red dress. My father had bought this dress for me about one year ago. It was a red velvet dress that I had picked out the last time that he took me shopping. The dress had short sleeves and two sexy slits on each side.

I picked up my black patent leather shoes from the bottom of the closet. I had already showered. I slipped on the sleek, red velvet dress, as I proudly looked into the full-length mirror. WOW! This dress really showed off my curves. I was surprised that I could still fit into the dress. As a matter of fact, the dress fit me better than ever. I calmly put on my shoes, fixed my hair in a nice French roll, and added the finishing touches to my make-up.

I picked up the telephone and called a cab to take me to the car rental agency. I was dressed to kill. As I entered the car rental agency, I noticed a tall, thin white man with white hair standing at the back of the counter. He appeared weary from a long, hard day of car rental customer service. "BOB" read the name tag pinned to his white dress shirt.

"Hello," I stated as I walked up to the front desk. "I would like to rent a car for the weekend."

"Well, young lady," he cheerfully responded, "we only have one car left. As a matter of fact, consider yourself lucky. Someone just canceled a reservation just one hour ago. We have a red 1989 Maxima, fully loaded."

WOW . . . I was so preoccupied with spying on Keno that I did not even think about making a reservation.

"Well, sir, how much would it cost to rent the vehicle for the weekend?" I asked with a subtle grin.

"Two hundred fifty dollars," he replied as he gestured a crooked smile. "You will need a valid credit card, along with a valid driver's license."

Valid credit cards were no problem for me. After all, I had every credit card that you could think of with limits exceeding $3,500.00 each. Pretty good for a college student. It seemed like all of us college students at Wagner College had no problem getting credit cards.

"No problem," I replied as I handed him my Visa card and driver's license. It seemed like the process of renting a car was taking so long, although I had only been at the rental agency for about fifteen minutes. Finally, after thirty minutes of him verifying all of my information, Bob approached me waiting at the counter.

"It all checks out good," he stated as he handed me back my driver's license and credit card. "I'll drive it around, and you'll be set to take the vehicle."

As I walked outside, around to the back of the building, Bob drove up in the glossy red Maxima. It was even more beautiful than I had imagined, almost matching the exact color of my red velvet dress.

"Well," stated Bob as he hopped out of the car, "she's all yours. All of your paperwork is here—I just need your signature. The car is due back by twelve noon on Sunday."

"Thank you," I replied as I quickly signed my name on the receipts.

"Have a good time," shouted Bob as I drove the car out of the lot.

The vehicle was so beautiful. As I sat in the car, I changed the radio station to many different stations. After about five minutes of trying to find the best music to listen to, I finally found a song that was appealing to my ears. One hour had already passed by since I had spoken to Sheba. After all of the time that I had spent renting the car, Sheba should have been dressed and ready to go. I drove down the spiral road, and spotted a payphone. I abruptly got out of the vehicle and dialed Sheba's telephone number.

"Hello."

"Hi, this is Sabrina, I picked up the rental, and I am on my way to pick you up from home."

"I should be ready in five minutes," stated Sheba in a loud tone of voice. "Sabrina, when you get in front of my house, just beep the horn, and I will come right downstairs."

"Okay," I replied.

"I will see you soon."

"Alright," I stated. I anxiously entered the vehicle. I thought to myself, wow, this is going to be a great night. I could not wait to get to the Underground Club. As I slowly drove up to Sheba's house, I noticed her standing outside. Sheba was dressed like she just walked out of a fashion plate magazine. She was attractive and always looked nice in her clothes. Although Sheba lived in an upper-middle class neighborhood, there were still people who lived there who I declared as "ghetto."

"Ooh girl, where are you going?" asked one of Sheba's nosy neighbors as she held a beer can up to her pale-brown face.

"I'm going out, somewhere you can't go," Sheba angrily stated as she got into the vehicle.

"Some things never change," I stated in an abrupt voice. "You can take some people out of the ghetto, but you can't take the ghetto out of some people." We both laughed.

"Hey, Sabrina, nice wheels you got here. We're riding in style."

"Yes, we certainly are. I was quite lucky. Someone canceled at the last minute, and here we are riding instead of taking the ferry and train."

Sheba and I were enjoying the scenery as we crossed the Verrazano Bridge. There was very little traffic on the highway. We were having a great time enjoying the music, and talking about the good old school days. Before I knew it, we were approaching the club. "UNDERGROUND" read the gold-glittered sign on the flat-top building.

"There goes the Club," shouted Sheba, as we parked the vehicle in front of the parking meter.

I began to feel afraid. Many questions began to run across my mind. What if I caught Keno in an act that he could not explain? What if he were upset that I even came to the club? How would I react if I saw something that I did not want to see? It was too late to turn back. I was already here. Sheba and I attempted to walk up to the front door of the Underground Club. We could hear the loud sound of the reggae music playing as we walked towards the back of the long line of about fifty people. Finally, the line got shorter after a twenty minute wait.

As Sheba and I approached the entrance, the bouncer asked, "ID, please, and the admission is ten dollars each." He was a short, stocky, fair-skinned young man about in his late twenties. He spoke with a slight lisp. I handed him my ID, and Sheba did the same. The bouncer shouted, "You two ladies can go in for free. Have a nice time tonight."

As we approached the entrance of the club I noticed the blue neon lights which illuminated the entire dance floor. The crowd was so dense, and we had to literally push our way over to the bar. I was so excited. The sound of the music slowly began to crowd my mind. I felt the beat of the music penetrate my soul. As we walked towards the bar, I heard a man order a drink.

"Vodka on the rocks, please." Ha, ha, ha shouted the two men that sat nearby.

As Sheba and I walked up to the bar, the bartender grudgingly asked, "What will you two ladies be drinking tonight?"

I responded, "I'll have an amaretto on the rocks." That was my favorite social drink.

"I'll have the same," replied Sheba. The room was dimly lit and the people who were sitting around the bar appeared to be too comfortable. They almost appeared to be permanent residents. They were probably sitting there all day. Sheba and I decided to get up from the bar with our drinks and walk around. As we were walking around the club, I looked to my left and noticed a young man and young lady dancing. He appeared to have her pinned to the wall. It almost seemed as if they were having sexual intercourse. As we walked further into the crowd, we could see many people intensely dancing to the beat of the music. They acted as if they were contestants in a dance contest, and they all had to win. As we approached the ramp, we entered into another area of the club.

Sheba shouted, "Hey, Sabrina, there's Keno." As she finished her statement I could feel my body run bitter-cold, as if a numbness took hold of me.

"Yeah, you're right. That is Keno." As I looked in the direction where Keno was, I noticed him standing there with two young men, and a female who appeared to have had trouble with keeping her hands away from Keno's face. I kept wondering if I should scream now, or wait until later. I figured that I would wait until later. Keno was going home with me tonight. As Sheba and I approached Keno and his boys, he glanced at me as if he had seen a ghost.

"Hello, Keno," I exclaimed. Sheba stood there next to me, speechless. Well, Keno was just too through with me. He looked at me as if he wanted to disappear. Before Keno could respond, the female who was standing with Keno and his friends abruptly slurred.

"Hey, Keno, who is she? When are we going to get up out of this place?" She was dressed in spiked-high heels, and wore half of a dress. She must have bought it at a half-price sale, I thought. She obviously had too much to drink. Before I could get a chance to verbally attack her, Keno shouted, "Yo, my girl is here. I will check you out some other time." I had to really ask myself what would have really happened if I did not show up at the club. I started to wonder if Keno would have cheated on me that night if I never showed up. A large part of me, deep down inside of me, gave him the benefit of the doubt and denied the truth—even when it stared me in the face. If I didn't catch him in the act, I never accused him. I was in denial. As she abruptly walked away, she blew Keno a kiss.

"So, Sabrina, what made you come here tonight? What did you expect to see? Did you find what you were looking for?"

The sound of the music became intensely louder. Although I was very upset, I could not show it. I felt as if I had to pretend that seeing him with someone else did not bother me.

"I just thought that I would surprise you, by meeting you here. I even rented a car. I hope that you are not upset, Keno." I always had a way of hoping, when it came to Keno. I was slowly beginning to realize that my insecurities from someplace deep in my subconscious were beginning to surface.

"Sabrina, I'm not upset at you. I'm just surprised to see you here, that's all." Keno appeared to be experiencing a slight anxiety attack, when all of a sudden he abruptly stated, "Sheba, let me introduce you to my long-time friend Marky. Marky, this is my girl, Sabrina. Sabrina, this is Marky."

"Nice meeting you," I softly stated.

Marky was a short, stocky young man. He sported a low-faded haircut. He held a drink in each hand, and spoke very loudly. "So, I have heard a lot about you, Sabrina, when is the wedding date?"

"Oh, I'm not really sure," I grudgingly replied. "Keno and I are in the process of discussing our future. Trust me, as soon as we set a date, you will be one of the first people to know."

"Oh, I just love Southern Comfort whiskey," shouted Marky as he walked towards the exit door of the club. I could literally smell the liquor seeping through the pores of his sweaty body. "Yeah, Sabrina, Marky is known for sweatin' the Southern Comfort." We all laughed.

"Well, we all need to be headed for home," said Keno. I

glanced at my watch. The time read 1:30 a.m. I was tired. I just wanted to go home and relax with Keno. Sheba drove the vehicle, while Keno and I sat in the back seat. Marky had hitched a ride with one of his cousins who was surprisingly sober. It seemed to be a long ride home, back to Staten Island. Everyone in the car was quiet. There was no music playing, no laughing, or talking. As we drove along the highways, Keno stared out of the window. I, on the other hand, was staring out of the window closest to me. I felt a calm and peaceful feeling as I glanced at the cars passing by. As we drove along the Verrazano Bridge, although it was dark, I noticed the tranquility of the water. The waves rippled peacefully. Before I knew it, Sheba was paying the toll in order to cross the bridge to Staten Island. After about twenty minutes, Sheba was finally driving up to Keno's house. I decided to stay over Keno's place, since it was so late. We were back in familiar territory. I was more than relieved.

"Thank you for driving back to Staten Island, Sheba."

"No problem, Sabrina," Sheba replied in her famous Jamaican country accent.

"You can keep the car until tomorrow. Just call me and we can both take it back tomorrow." I was just too tired and disgusted to prolong the conversation. I began slurring my speech.

"Good night," Keno exclaimed, "good night."

We both walked up to the front entrance of the house. Keno took out his bunch of keys and opened the door. We proceeded to walk up the stairs, with Keno leading the way. As we entered the front of the bedroom door, Keno pushed me into the door and onto the king-sized bed. Keno proceeded to take off all of my clothes. We kissed and he ran his hand down the side of my thigh. Before I knew it, we were making passionate love together. Wow, I thought, his expression towards me was worth more than words. Keno did not need to say "I love you." Why? Because I already knew. Keno and I fell fast asleep.

I was not too thrilled about Keno and I meeting up with Marky and his fiancée. Since Keno seemed so excited about us hanging out with Marky and his future wife, I made it my business to cooperate. It was a cool Friday evening when Keno and I met Marky and his fiancée at the famous Placid Restaurant. As Keno and I walked toward the restaurant, I could see Marky waving, attempting to get Keno's attention. Finally, Keno and Marky caught each other's attention.

"Well, hello," stated Marky as Keno and I approached the front entrance of the restaurant.

"Nice meeting you again," I replied.

"My fiancée is sitting over there waiting for us at the table." We all quickly walked over to the table where Marky's fiancée was seated. She appeared to be a slim-built female, with big brown eyes. Her complexion was light brown. Her eyes resembled two almonds. Her makeup looked too perfect for the occasion. I started to feel like one of her competitors in what would be a fashion show. She was dressed in a white laced blouse. What was I worried about? After all, I was only here to please my man, Keno. I just wanted the evening to quickly pass by. We were all seated at a round table. I could smell the aroma of the freshly picked flowers that were placed in the middle of the table. The glare of the candles that were on the table gave each of our faces a glow of mystery.

"So," exclaimed Marky, "this is my fiancée, Stephanie. Stephanie, this is my good friend, Keno, and his fiancée Sabrina."

"Hi, Sabrina, it's a pleasure to meet you," replied Stephanie in a country-southern accent. "I have heard so much about you, Sabrina, and I think that it is so sweet that you would just drop out of college and get a full time job, just to please your man. You're a good girl, because if I were in the private school that you are in—Wagner College—you know how many people would love to be in your shoes? The cost for one credit could buy me a condo."

Everyone chuckled, except me. All of a sudden, I felt the urge to get up and leave the restaurant. Instead, I kept my cool, and remained seated. I was very upset. Keno and I never came to a conclusion regarding my leaving college. Besides, she had the story all mixed up. I decided to have some fun, and play along with Keno's game. At least for the evening.

"Yeah, Stephanie," I replied, I am not actually leaving college, but I will be transferring to a City college, so that I may work full time during the day, and go to school part-time during the evening."

"Yes," replied Keno, "Sabrina is doing a great thing. We would be able to save some money together so that we could get an apartment. I am looking forward to spending the future with Sabrina."

"That's cool," stated Marky as the waiter approached our table.

"So, what can I get you all to drink?"

"We will have a pitcher of cola, if you don't mind," said Keno. We all agreed to order a variety of Buffalo wings. After all, I was in no mood to eat. I really just wanted to get home, in order to confront Keno concerning my transferring from Wagner College. There was silence during most of the time that we were eating dinner. I had made up my mind that I would not have much of anything to say, until I got home. As we were finishing our meal, the waiter brought the check.

"Is there anything else I can bring out for you all?"

"No, that would be all," exclaimed Keno as he took his credit card out of his wallet. "It's on me." We all got up from the table, and walked towards the exit.

"Keno," stated Marky, "thanks for coming out to have a bite to eat with us. I really appreciate you and Sabrina's company."

"Take care," shouted Stephanie as we walked out of the restaurant. We walked out into the parking lot, and got into Keno's vehicle.

"Keno, we need to talk about a few issues concerning my leaving Wagner College."

"I know, Sabrina, as soon as we get home, I would like us to have a nice long talk."

We arrived at home within a half hour. We both changed our clothes into matching sweat suits that we bought from The Big Apple Bazaar.

"Sabrina, I just want to let you know that I really love you, and I'm looking forward to us being together for the rest of our lives," stated Keno as he embraced me closely.

"Keno," I replied, as I abruptly moved away from him, "we need to be on the same page regarding our future. First, you tell your mother that I'm leaving school, without even discussing the issue with me. Today, while we were out with Marky and Stephanie, I had to listen to her go on and on about how she heard that I was leaving school. Keno, why didn't you discuss this issue with me before you told everyone that I was leaving school, in order to get a full time job?" Keno looked at me as if he were surprised that I actually was questioning him.

"Sabrina, I did not intend on offending you at all. If I did, I apologize. I just wanted to be positive by claiming the desire that I have for you to cooperate with the plans that I made for our future." That was the problem. Keno was making the plans for our future alone. I came too far into this relationship in order to disagree with Keno.

61

"Well, Sabrina, you wouldn't believe. Do you remember the Director of Personnel from the agency that I work for?"

"No, not really," I replied.

"Mr. Greenstein, the one with all of the power. I told him all about you. You know, how smart you are, and that you need to gain a full time position within the company, and that we were engaged to become married. He was really receptive. You know what, Sabrina, he even scheduled an interview for you on next Thursday, at 1:00 p.m."

I started to feel trapped—like a little girl left home all alone, sitting in a playpen. I did not have the strength to tell Keno that I would not accept his offer to go to the interview. I felt obligated to cooperate, even though I did not want to. I was eager to finish the conversation. I perceived that I had to remain calm and agree to his protocol, not realizing or caring how dangerous this situation could become.

"Okay, Keno, that sounds really exciting. Give me the information so that I can prepare myself."

About one week had passed, and it was the day before the interview was scheduled. Although I was not too thrilled about going to the interview, I found enough courage to convince myself that this was the correct path to follow. I had forced myself to become so excited about the situation. I decided to visit my mother in order to share the good news. It was a cold, dark, gloomy evening when I went to visit my mother. As I rode up the elevator to the seventh floor, I began to feel a slight sense of urgency to appear into my mother's presence. As the elevator ascended to the seventh floor, I became anxious. I stepped out of the elevator, and knocked on the door, "7C." My mother had the usual shrewd look on her face.

"Hi, Sabrina," exclaimed my mother. She appeared to be quite content on this cloudy evening. It was evident that the good news that I was going to give her concerning my decision to get a full time job would make her even more proud of me.

"Come in, sit down, don't act like a stranger." I sat down in my usual chair, the suede, yellow rocking chair that my sister and I fought over for many of our childhood years. The chair had a permanent impression of both of our gerri-curl hair activated-gel hairstyles from the early 1980's. It was evident that we had spent a lot of time sitting in the yellow rocking chair.

My mother was always receptive to listening to my problems. I had a lot of respect for her and always took her advice as needed. I was hoping that my mother would tell me what my ears wanted to hear.

Either way, I would take her advice regarding my situation. I always respected my mother's opinion.

"Hello, Sabrina," said my mother with a calm look on her pre-senior aged face.

"Hey mom, what's up?" I replied. I always wanted my mother to believe that everything in my life was going perfectly, even if it wasn't. For some strange reason, I was always able to hide the truth regarding what was really always going on in my drama-filled life. I believe that my mother always knew what was really going on, but never exposed it. She was a woman that I always looked up to. She was the true PROVERBS woman that the Bible book of Proverbs literally bragged about.

"Mom, I just wanted to let you know that Keno landed me a really great job. He knows this 'big wig' that oversees a department within the organization that he works for. *Can you believe it?*" I exclaimed in a loud voice. "He was actually able to land me a job interview. I plan on transferring to a CUNY school. I could go to school part-time during the evening. I could work full-time during the day. Just think of it, Keno and I could move into our own apartment together, and plan for our future."

Based on my performance in the presence of my mother, I convinced myself into believing that I was making the right decision regarding my plans to be with Keno in the future. The expression that was on my mother's face was worth more than words. She appeared to have lost her best friend in an unfortunate battle.

"Sabrina," my mother softly stated, "I understand that you really love Keno, but let me be honest with you." My mother's voice became louder and stronger. "You have one year left before you graduate from college. Sabrina, do you remember how excited you were when you first got accepted to Wagner College? Do you remember how many of your classmates that you grew up with, here in the Stapleton Projects, got the opportunity like you did to get into a school like that?"

I began to remember that nobody in my class actually received the opportunity that I had. I began to wonder if I was actually crazy for even considering going along with Keno's plan.

"If Keno really loved you, he would wait until you graduate. You only have one year before you graduate. Sabrina, I love you, and you know this. I really want the best for you. Let me say this also. If you leave that school, and go along with Keno's plan, you will be the sorriest black woman that ever walked the earth."

As usual, I always respected whatever my mother told me whenever she gave me advice. There was something different about the tone of her voice *this time*. I clearly heard the sense of urgency in her voice. I had no choice but to take her advice. I was still going to play Keno's game by going to the job interview that he had already set up, just for his sake.

"Mom, I sincerely would like to thank you so much for your advice."

"You are very welcome, Sabrina. I just really hope that you take my advice to heart."

"I will, Mom," I stated as I kissed her on her rosy colored high-boned cheek and got up in order to walk towards the double-lock bolted front door.

"Well, Mom, I will speak to you soon, again thanks, and I love you." Well, that was easy enough, I thought, well at least on the surface. At this point, I was starting to feel confused. I was confused about everything. Would I be making the right choice by even going to the interview? If I didn't go to the interview, how would that make Keno feel? Did I really want to go to the interview at all? These were some of the many questions that began to surface.

As I approached the house where Keno and I resided along with his family, I began to feel sick to my stomach. I walked up the steps, and unlocked the weather-beaten front door. Before I could enter the door, I noticed Keno, standing there with three helium-filled balloons. "Congratulations" read the bold letters on the balloons. I was so startled, I did not say a word.

"Hey, Sabrina, many congratulations to you on your new job. I know that you did not go to the interview yet, but I know that you are going to ace that interview. That's a given. I know that Mr. Greenstein is going to hire you."

"Thanks for the encouragement, Keno," I stated as I blew him a kiss.

"So, Sabrina, are you nervous about the interview?"

"No way," I stated in a low but coy voice. "I still have some time to prepare myself. It's Wednesday, and tomorrow is the interview," I nervously replied.

"You know something, Sabrina, this interview means a lot to me. It's actually going to determine our future together. As I mentioned before, we will be able to save money, so that we could move in together and prepare for our future. I have even prepared myself to purchase you a more expensive ring."

It suddenly occurred to me that Keno and I were on different pages of life. We were speaking different languages. Even though I noticed the differences in our mind-sets, I was not prepared to let him go, or disappoint him. I decided to play his game, as long as I could last.

It was a beautiful Thursday morning, the day of my interview. The weather was warm, and the sun was shining brightly. When I opened the window, I could feel the warm breeze brush across my face. The aroma of the freshly-cut grass filled my nostrils. Keno was getting ready for work, and I had decided not to go to any classes on that particular day. I just wanted to get the interview over and done with. It was about nine o'clock in the morning. Keno was obviously running late for work.

"Okay, Sabrina," stated Keno as he rushed down the stairs, "good luck at the interview. Call me at the office when you're finished. The address and directions to the interview are right there on the table."

"Okay," I replied, in a mono-toned voice. I began to feel nervous about the whole situation. I decided to take my shower, and prepare myself for the interview. Finally, I was dressed. I wore a white business-style shirt, with a navy blue knee-length skirt. My shoes were just right for the occasion. They were a pair of casual black penny-loafers. As soon as I was dressed, I called a cab to the Staten Island Ferry. The boat ride was very relaxing. "Lady Liberty" appeared to be more glamorous standing under the grey clouds in the middle of the harbor. Although I was enjoying the boat ride, it seemed as if the ride was a little longer than usual. As we approached the harbor in Manhattan, the boat made its faithful, loud bump into the logs on the pier. Everyone walked off the ferry as if they had someplace important to go, except for me. I strolled off the boat like I had all day to reach my destination. After all, it was only 11:30 in the morning. I arrived at the #1 train station, and waited on the platform with about fifty other straphangers. After about four stops on the train, I finally reached my destination.

"Next stop, Franklin Street," stated the train conductor in a loud, raspy voice.

I got up, and walked up onto the street level. The address that I was looking for was 455 Franklin Street. I walked down the crowded, busy street, and on the left side of the street was the building. I decided to "kill some time" by going over to the diner on the corner for a cup of coffee and a doughnut. Finally it was 12:30. I abruptly walked out of the diner, over to 455 Franklin Street. As I approached the skyscraper-styled building, the security guard stared at me, as if I were an unexpected visitor. I proceeded to walk over to the elevators, when he stopped me.

He was a tall, white man who appeared to have had no sleep within the past two days.

"Excuse me, miss, do you have an appointment to see someone in the building?"

"Yes, I'm scheduled to interview with Mr. Greenstein," I stated as I reached in my tote bag and pulled out a crumpled piece of paper containing the information regarding the interview.

"What floor is he on?" asked the guard.

"He's on the fifth floor; I believe he's with the Parking Violations Bureau," I stated.

"Oh, yes, you're absolutely correct," the man stated as he browsed through a black and white marble notebook. "I will just need to see a piece of identification."

I showed the man my driver's license.

"You can go up to the fifth floor, over there," he stated as he pointed to a pair of elevators. "Good luck on your interview," he yelled as he turned away from me.

The rickety elevator doors opened and I pressed #5. The door opened, and I noticed a bright sign which read: PARKING VIOLATIONS BUREAU. I got off the elevator and walked towards a woman who was seated at a desk. She was a dark-skinned woman who was dressed in what appeared to be business-casual attire. I assumed that she was Mr. Greenstein's secretary.

"Hi, may I help you?" she politely asked.

"Yes, I am here for an interview. I believe it's for the data entry position."

"What is your name?" she demanded.

"Sabrina. Sabrina Matheson."

"Oh, yes," she stated as she looked over a long white sheet of paper containing about fifty names. "Just sit right here," she stated as she pointed to the set of chairs that was positioned directly across from her. "Mr. Greenstein will be right with you."

I began to feel nervous. After waiting about ten minutes, my palms began to sweat. Finally, Mr. Greenstein appeared. He was a heavy set white man, who appeared to be in his mid-fifties. He wore a black yarmulke on the crown of his head. The hair on the sides of his head was white. His moustache and beard were a perfect match. His white shirt appeared to have been abused by the sweat, caused by the previous summers.

"Hi, Sabrina," he stated as if he had known me for years. "I'm glad to see that you showed up for the interview early. That's a plus in my book. Just for the record, Keno already sent me your resume. I was very impressed with your work history, and present educational background. I just wanted to place the face with the resume," he cunningly stated. "The job is yours," he cheerfully shouted. "Would you be able to start on Monday?"

I suddenly began to feel as if Keno had set me up. This was no interview. This was just an arrangement that Keno had made behind my back for selfish reasons. I had made up my mind that I was not going to take the job. I would not tell Mr. Greenstein, but I would tell Keno when I got back to the house.

"I would be able to start on next Thursday, Mr. Greenstein," I stated as I glared at the brightly colored still-life painting that was hanging on the withered wall.

"That would be great, Sabrina. When you come in next Thursday, please be here at 8:30 a.m. You will also need to bring your original birth certificate and Social Security card. If you have a driver's license, it would be a good idea if you also bring it."

"Okay, Mr. Greenstein, I will see you next week. Thank you for your time."

"I will see you soon, Sabrina."

It was a long ride back home on the train and the ferry. It seemed as if the people had nothing else better to do than overcrowd the train's platform. I was mentally preparing myself for telling Keno that I would not take the position that Mr. Greenstein offered me. I kept hearing my mother's voice saying, "If you transfer from Wagner College to a City school, you will be the sorriest black woman that ever walked this earth. If Keno really cared about you, he would wait." It seemed as if the closer I got back to the house, the louder her voice became. Finally, I reached back to our place. When I entered into the house, Keno was sitting in the living room. He had a look on his face that I could not describe.

"Hey, Sabrina, how's it going? How did the interview

go?" he asked, in a tone as if he had known all along that I landed the position.

"Keno, there are some things that I need to discuss with you regarding this whole situation."

"What is it, Sabrina," Keno abruptly exclaimed as he crossed his muscular arms.

"I really don't think that I should take the job. As a matter of fact, I'm not going to accept the position. I mean, Keno, if you really cared about me, you would wait for me. I'm a junior, for God's sake. Next year I am going to graduate. You know that graduating from this school is very important to me. Also, if I transfer, I will lose credits."

"Sabrina, what the hell are you in a rush to graduate for?" Keno shouted in a harsh, angry monotone voice. "Sabrina, you act as if you are in a race to get out of college in four years. Nobody's in a race around here."

"I'm sorry, Keno, I just can't do it. My mother even agrees that if I did take the position, and work full time, I'd be making the wrong choice."

"What the hell does your mother have to do with this?" Keno frantically exclaimed. "She's not the one supporting you. I am. And you know something, Sabrina, it's getting a little bit too expensive. As a matter of fact, I don't want to do this anymore. You made me believe that you were in my corner. You made me go out of my way to convince Mr. Greenstein that you were perfect for the position that he interviewed you for. The engagement is off."

As I attempted to grab Keno by the arm, he quickly ran out of the house and slammed the door.

Three hours passed since I had seen Keno at the house. It was about eight o'clock in the evening when I finally fell asleep. I got up the next morning, and got dressed for class. Keno was still not at home. I decided to pretend like we never had a disagreement. I spent the day just as I always did. I focused on my classes, enjoyed conversation with my class-mates, and spent some time in the library. I was feeling like I really wanted to see Keno. In fact, I could not wait until I got home so that we could make up, and start all over again. Even though he said that the engagement was off, I still had hope. For some strange reason, I did not believe him.

I had finished my research at the library early. As I got off the bus, on the way to Keno's house where we resided together, I began to feel a sense of sadness. As I approached the house, I noticed a pile of clothes in the front of the house from a distance. As I got closer to the pile of clothing, I began to realize that the clothes belonged to me. Keno had literally dumped all of my clothes outside. I took out my keys in order to open the door, and surprisingly, my keys would not open the door. Keno had changed the locks. I began to feel a huge anxiety attack come upon me. I knocked on the neighbor's door and asked to use the phone. I picked up the telephone, anticipating that I would speak with Keno. The phone rang many times, and nobody answered. I called Sheba. Thank God that she was home.

"Sheba," I exclaimed in the middle of my sobbing, "it's a long story, and I can't even think right now. Keno broke off the engagement because I wouldn't take the job, and transfer schools. My clothes are all outside in the front of the house. I am at Ms. Yona's house next door."

"I'll be right over," Sheba screamed in a frantic voice, and slammed down the phone.

I was sobbing uncontrollably. "He threw my clothes outside, like I'm a dog, he didn't love me, there must be somebody else."

"Oh, my goodness," shouted the neighbor. "Is there something that I can do for you, Sabrina? This is so terrible. It will be okay," stated Ms. Yona.

Ms. Yona was an oriental woman who appeared to be in her mid-fifties. She's a neighbor who always said "good morning" when the morning wasn't going so good. She seemed like a nice person who was always polite. This was one day that I really appreciated Ms. Yona's kindness. She made me a cup of tea, and allowed me to wait in her home until Sheba would arrive. I was slowly beginning to finally realize that my world with Keno had collapsed right before my eyes. The anxiety that I was beginning to perceive regarding the situation was beginning to overwhelm me. I began to feel like I had lost my only connection to true life, and true love. It seemed as if Sheba was taking a long time to get to Ms. Yona's house. I didn't have any words for conversation. I just sat quietly and waited for Sheba.

I sat by the large storm window in the living room. Ms. Yona's living room reminded me of a museum. She had very colorful paintings that appeared to be very expensive hanging on the walls. There were many glass items neatly placed in the wall unit. The tiles were made of heavy ceramic. I was constantly glancing into the front yard in great expectation of Sheba's arrival. It was as if I were a child, desperately waiting for my mother to pick me up from aftercare.

After about an hour, I noticed Sheba walk up to Ms. Yona's front door. She did not have on her best Sunday attire, but I was still glad to see her. She came to my rescue. I abruptly ran outside into the front yard in order to meet her.

"Sheba," I stated as I began to sob, "the wedding is off. Keno wants nothing to do with me. Look over there," I yelled as I pointed to the pile of clothes that were in the front yard next door. "Those are all of my clothes. He basically threw me out. I can't even get into the house," I screamed as I hastily threw the engagement ring into the bushes nearby.

"Where did all of this confusion come from?" Sheba hastily questioned.

As I attempted to explain myself, I noticed Keno drive up into the driveway, with his mother Ms. Williams in the front seat. She glanced at me and quickly turned away. As Keno got out of the vehicle, Sheba attempted to get his attention.

"Keno, may I speak with you?" Sheba politely asked.

"Right now, I don't have the time," he abruptly stated as he entered into the house.

As Ms. Williams was getting out of Keno's vehicle, she put on her sunglasses. She appeared to have something very important to say, but was obviously having a difficult time. Finally, she got up enough nerve and spoke.

"Sabrina, I'm very sorry about what has happened. You can stay here until you get yourself together."

"Just like that?" I questioned in a desperate tone of voice. "Can't you talk to him? He won't even speak to me," I stated in a tremored voice.

"You know, Sabrina, Keno wants other things out of life. That's all I can say," she stated in a tone of voice which indicated that I had been set up all along.

As a result of the stress that I was experiencing, I could feel the blood in my veins starting to boil. It seemed as if Ms. Williams finally got the revenge that she always wanted. Keno and I were history. Sheba and I began to swiftly pick up my clothes, and bring them into the front room of the house. After all of the clothes were piled up in the front room, Sheba and I sat in the living room.

"Sabrina, I just want you to know that this is not going to be easy for you. I want you to know that I'm here for you." Even though I found her words to be quite soothing, I was too upset to even reply.

"Now you have to focus on moving forward. I'm not really

clear on what happened here, but it's not making any sense to me." As Sheba finished her sentence, Keno walked down the stairs, and out of the house. I felt the immediate urge to get up and run after him, but I didn't. Ms. Williams entered into the room where we were seated, and joined our conversation.

"Sabrina," stated Ms. Williams, "you can stay here, as I told you, until you get everything in order. As far as Keno is concerned, I already told you, he wants other things."

I was starting to believe that Ms. Williams was hiding something. She wanted me there for her convenience, but offered no sympathy for what I was experiencing.

"I'll just sit here for awhile, and then I will go back to my mother's house."

"Okay," replied Ms. Williams, "whatever you say," she stated in a monotone voice. "Sabrina, you are always welcome in my home. You can always visit whenever you like."

I was starting to believe that Ms. Williams was actually crazy.

"Well, I will be going," she yelled as she approached the front door in order to leave. "Before you go, just slam the door, and it will lock."

Sheba and I sat on the couch in silence. Finally, the silence was broken.

"Sabrina, I am so sorry that this has happened to you."

"I know, Sheba, things happen in life, you know." I was trying to be strong but deep down inside, I felt as if I were breaking apart.

"If you like, Sabrina, I will bring your clothes to your mother's house."

"Thanks, just tell my mother that you're dropping off my clothes. You don't have to get into any details. I will explain everything to her when I get home."

Sheba hastily finished packing the clothes, and walked out

of the front door. I wasn't sure if she had slam-locked the door. Basically I didn't care. When I heard the engine of her vehicle fade away, I walked into the kitchen, and sat by the window. I began to recall the great times that Keno and I had. I began to regret even turning down the position that Mr. Greenstein offered me. I began to regret ever even meeting Keno. I began to regret everything. I began to regret ever being born. The pain that I was experiencing was too much to bear. I figured that I'd end it. I noticed a butcher knife on the counter. As I looked over on the refrigerator, I noticed a telephone number. It was Marky's number. I grabbed the knife and began to run it across my left wrist. I figured for some strange reason that before I ended my life, I would call Marky and tell him what happened between Keno and I. I had never called him in the past. I hardly knew him. I figured that it would be beneficial. My hands were shaking as I picked up the phone, in order to dial Marky's number. The phone rang, and finally someone answered. It was Marky.

"Hello, this is Marky."

"Hello, Marky, this is Sabrina, Keno's friend."

"Hi, Sabrina, how's everything?" he asked in a tone as if he had already known about our break-up.

"I just want you to know that Keno and I broke up, and I'm not taking it too well. I thought that I would be able to handle the pressure, but I'm having a really hard time dealing with this situation. I know that I only met you twice, but you are his friend, and I needed to talk to somebody about it."

"Sabrina, you have to move on. Don't let this ruin your future. You seem to be a very nice girl."

"You know what, Marky," I stated as I ran the knife back and forth across my wrist, "I think I'm going to kill myself."

"No, Sabrina, don't do it. I'm coming right over," Marky yelled in a tone of voice as if he were actually expecting me to tell him that I was going to kill myself. Marky slammed down the phone.

I held the knife in my hand, negotiating with myself whether I should slit my wrist or not. Still holding the knife, I began to cry, and ask myself why I was ever born. After about fifteen minutes of negotiating with myself, the front door flew open. I could hear someone running towards the back of the house, into the kitchen where I was sitting with the knife in my hand rocking back and forth. It was Marky. Apparently Sheba did not slam-lock the door when she left the house.

"Sabrina, put the knife down," he screamed as he lunged towards me and snatched the knife out of my hand. "This is crazy," exclaimed Marky, "I'm going to call 911."

"No, please don't do that. I'm going over to my mother's house. I will be okay."

"Sabrina, I'm not going to let you leave this house until you promise me that you will not kill yourself."

"I promise." I was starting to feel like I had developed another personality. Just one minute ago, I was planning to slit my wrist. While talking with Marky, I was a "level-headed" person. Was I going crazy?

"Sabrina, let me drive you over to your mother's house."

I slowly got up off of the wooden chair. Marky took hold of my arm, and led me to the front door, as if I were a helpless person who could not find her way home.

The ride to my mother's house was very quick. I was able to give Marky the shortcut streets to take, despite the negative state of mind that I was experiencing. As I was getting out of the vehicle, Marky gave me a military handshake. I was glad to be back at my mother's house. In a sense, I still felt as if what had happened between Keno and I was all a bad dream. I was hoping that I'd wake up and everything would be perfect between Keno and I.

Eight days had passed by since I had spoken to Keno. I never told my mother that I had thoughts of killing myself. I only told her what I wanted her to know. I told her that we decided not to stay together, because we had different ideas about how we should plan our future. I had not returned calls that Sheba had made to me, all week. I had purposely made myself unavailable to family, friends and classmates. I was avoiding everyone. I preferred to stay at home. The only time that I saw sunlight was when I went to classes.

On one dreary Thursday evening, I decided to call Keno. I needed to speak to him. I needed to see his face. As I picked up the telephone, I began to recall the good times that Keno and I shared together. I wanted to relive those times again. I dialed the number, hoping that he would answer the phone. Finally, after the phone rang about four times, Keno picked up the phone.

"Hello."

"Hi, Keno, this is Sabrina. I need to see you."

"For what?" Keno angrily replied. "I thought I told you that it was over."

I began to feel as if I were in a desperate state.

"I know, but I just need to see you. I'm not trying to make you do anything you don't want to. I just need to see you."

"Marky told me that you tried to hurt yourself."

"No, I wasn't going to do it. I was just feeling very upset at the time. I'm still upset, but I think that if I see you, I would feel much better."

"Okay," Keno replied. "Where are you, at your mother's?"

"Yes," I replied.

"I'm just telling you, Sabrina, I'm going to come talk to you, but I can't stay long. I'm only doing this because you want me to."

I wanted to scream after I heard Keno's words. I felt like

someone had just thrown an arrow into my heart. I felt betrayed.

"Sabrina, I'm going to drive in front of your mother's house. Please be in front of the building in twenty minutes."

"Okay," I replied.

Fifteen minutes had passed by. I decided to go downstairs and wait for Keno in front of the building. After ten minutes of waiting, I noticed Keno driving up to the building where I was standing. Keno was not driving his car. I was surprised to see him drive a new car, a shiny new grey sports car. The front of the car had headlights that resembled human eyes. He waved, capturing my attention, in order to confirm that it was he who was actually driving the vehicle that was foreign to me.

When we were together, as I recalled, he never had any plans to buy a new vehicle. As he approached where I was standing, I walked over to the passenger's side seat, and got into the vehicle. The car had a clean fresh smell, just like it was brand new. I glanced out of the window, hoping that Keno did not notice the tears that were in my eyes.

"So, hello Sabrina, how have you been? We can sit here and talk. I only have a few minutes."

"Keno, I really can't understand why we're not together."

"Sabrina, I gave you a chance. I thought that you really loved me."

"So, Keno, you wait until we break up and for celebration purposes, you buy a new car?" I angrily questioned as I inspected the back seat of the car.

"Sabrina, I had plans to buy this vehicle for us. I was just waiting for us to move in together, into our own apartment. Since our relationship didn't work out, I just decided to purchase it early."

For some strange reason, something just didn't sound sincere. At this point I didn't elaborate about Keno's explanation nor care about Keno purchasing the car. I just wanted Keno to give our relationship another chance.

"Keno, I still love you. I want us to be together."

"Sabrina, we could never rekindle our relationship. I've moved on with my life. I have other things that I'm doing with my life," he abruptly stated as he glanced at his watch, as if he were late for a dental appointment. At this point, I was so hurt that I didn't even respond. We sat in the vehicle silent for about ten minutes, until Keno broke the silence.

"Well, Sabrina, I need to be on my way."

I wanted to ask him where he was going, but instead I cooperated.

"Okay, Keno," I replied, as I quickly exited the car. I slammed the door, vowing never to look back. I felt like I had no control over what happened, and what was happening. I went upstairs into my room, and turned on the television. As I laid my head down on the pillow, the phone rang. It was Sheba.

"Hi, Sabrina, where you been girl?" she asked in her familiar Jamaican country accent.

"Well, Sheba," I've been taking it easy, and studying for my finals."

"Sabrina, I'm tired of you being depressed and moping all of the time. You have also been avoiding me. I know what I'm going to do. I'm going to contact your father, Mr. Barnes. I still have his number at the barber shop. I'm going to ask him if he would pay your way to come with me in August to Jamaica to visit my family. I'm going for two weeks."

"No, Sheba, really, that's okay. I don't feel like traveling nor being around people," I softly stated.

Sheba yelled, "You need to get away from Staten Island for awhile. You need a change of scenery. Keno has put a lot of stress on you. I think that you need to get away so that you could relax and calm your nerves. I'm going to call your father, Mr. Barnes." Before I could respond, Sheba had already hung up the phone. I really didn't want my father to know my business concerning Keno and I. Although I didn't spend a lot of time with my father, he was still supportive, whenever I did.

Shortly after I spoke with Sheba, the telephone rang again. It was my father, Mr. Barnes, who was on the phone.

"Hi, Sabrina, your friend Sheba called me, and she told me that you and your fiancée Keno broke up." He certainly was an expert on getting straight to the point. "How are you feeling?"

"I'm okay," I replied in a monotone voice.

"Sheba and I spoke about your going to Jamaica, West Indies with her in order to visit her family. We both know that you would benefit greatly if you went away with her for two weeks. Sheba told me how much it would cost for you to travel with her. I would love to pay for you to go."

I really was not in the mood to speak to my father about Keno. Neither was I interested in going away with Sheba to Jamaica. I didn't want to hurt my father's feelings, since his heart was set on helping me deal with Keno and I breaking up. I realized that he was only expressing concern for the trauma that I was experiencing, so I decided to accept his heartfelt offer.

"Okay, Dad, I will go to Jamaica with Sheba."

"Sabrina, I want you to hold your head up high. Don't be ashamed. You can use this experience in order to push forward, and become successful in life. Don't worry, one day you will meet the right man who will appreciate you for who you are, and what you believe in."

"Thanks, Dad, I really appreciate your support."

"Okay, Sabrina, you are very welcome. I will make arrangements with Sheba to pay for your airfare and hotel."

As I hung up the phone I began to picture in my mind what the island of Jamaica would look like. I pictured vibrant palm trees, blowing in the warm air. I imagined the beautiful waves in the water, glistening under the blue skies. Although I was beginning to look forward to putting Keno behind me, and stepping out into my new world, I was ready to suppress all of the hurt that I was feeling and pretend as if all of this never happened. I planned to use the vacation with Sheba as an escape from the pain, and the reality of Keno and I breaking up. I was becoming desperate to get away, so that I could purposely remove anything that reminded me of Keno. I started to pack my suitcase for my trip to Jamaica.

A week had already passed since I had spoken to Sheba or my father. I was finally starting to feel less anxiety regarding Keno. It was a cloudy Sunday morning when I decided to call Sheba.

"Hi, Sheba, this is Sabrina. Did you speak to my father, Mr. Barnes, regarding the vacation?"

"Yes, Sabrina, as a matter of fact, I was going to call you tonight, in order to tell you that your father paid for your airfare and hotel. He told me to tell you that he sent one thousand dollars for your spending money via Western Union."

"Wow," I exclaimed. "That is a lot of money." I started picturing myself further away from the pain of breaking up with Keno. "Well, Sheba, when are we leaving?"

"We are scheduled to leave in two weeks, on August 4th. The flight will be leaving the airport at 7:00 o'clock in the morning. We should reach Jamaica by 9:30 in the morning."

"I will continue to pack my bags. Mom also thinks that it would be a great idea if I went away for awhile."

"Sabrina, we are going to have a great time. My family would be happy to meet you."

"Well, Sheba, now that classes are over, I'm even more

excited about our vacation. I will call you later."

The days began to quickly pass by, bringing us closer to the date of our trip to Jamaica. The day of our getaway had finally arrived. It was a very humid Sunday morning, when Sheba and I met at the airport. I had packed my nicest summer outfits along with the best sandals that I had owned. The taxi ride to the airport went by quicker than I had imagined. As I approached the airport I noticed the huge planes taking off into the sky, which reminded me of a miracle. The enormous size of the planes prompted me to praise man for inventing the formula to safely fly a machine that large and complex around the world. I was looking forward to flying away on the plane, even though I was going to unfamiliar territory. At this point, I was willing to take any risk of getting away, and forgetting about Keno.

Sheba and I were enjoying the flight to Jamaica. We watched several movies, and enjoyed a full course meal. Finally, we arrived at the Montego Bay airport. As we departed the plane, women dressed in fancy skirts gave us a glass of rum punch and welcomed us to the island of Jamaica.

"Wow, Sheba," I exclaimed, "this is even more beautiful than I had ever imagined."

The weather was quite warm, and the people appeared as if they did not have a care in the world. The deep blue reflection of the ocean made my eyes tear. The sun beamed down on my light-brown streaked hair, as we walked towards the taxi-stand.

"Taxi-driver," stated Sheba, in her well-known country Jamaican accent, "we need a ride into town. We would like to go to the Jamaica Inn."

"Okay," the driver politely replied, "that will cost you forty U.S. dollars."

As we got into the taxi, and packed our luggage into the trunk of the vehicle, I began to wonder how this visit to

Jamaica would turn out after all. The ride to the hotel was pleasant. The driver told us jokes for most of the ride. It was obvious that he wanted to make us happy. I noticed cows grazing along the countryside. The ocean waves were so beautiful; only an imagination could actually interpret their rhythms. The palm trees that were withered as a result of the Gilbert storm peacefully blew in the trade winds. I felt as if I were in paradise.

During the first week of our vacation, Sheba and I enjoyed many water sports, going dancing, relaxing at the beach, and meeting her cousins who lived on the island. I was not thinking about Keno, at least while I was in Jamaica. I felt as if I had successfully forgotten about all of the pain and hurt that Keno had caused me. We had one more week to spend in Jamaica. I was having the time of my life.

One Tuesday afternoon, while we were out shopping, Sheba decided to take me to meet her Aunt Dora at work. It was quite a long walk from the shopping area. The rays of the sun made me feel faint. Finally, we approached the restaurant. "The Rapids Restaurant" read the tapered neon sign that hung above the front window. As we approached the front entrance of the restaurant, a young man, who appeared to be in his mid-thirties, greeted us.

"Come in; welcome to the Rapids. You may be seated anywhere you like. Make yourself at home."

Sheba and I picked a cozy seat facing the front entrance. The décor of the restaurant reminded me of the funk era of the 1970's.

"Hi, waiter," stated Sheba, as she put the menu into the center of the wicker table. "I'm looking for my Aunt Dora; she works here. Would you be kind enough to check and see if she's here now?"

"Oh, Dora, that's your auntie? She's a nice woman. She

makes me laugh a lot. She has a good sense of humor. Look here, let me go and check. Me soon come back."

After about five minutes, a woman abruptly walked up to our table. She was a fair-skinned woman with black and grey Shirley Temples in her hair. She seemed quite friendly and spoke with a soft voice. She wore a white dress with a pink scarf around her neck.

"Sheba," the woman exclaimed as she tightly hugged Sheba. "So how's life in the States?"

"Life is good," replied Sheba. "This is my best friend, Sabrina. Sabrina, this is my Aunt Dora."

"Pleased to meet you, Sabrina," Dora stated as she mysteriously glanced towards the front door.

"I brought Sabrina to our hometown so that she could have some fun."

"Oh, don't worry, darling, you will have fun while you're here, because here in Jamaica, there's no problem." We all chuckled. We sat together for awhile talking about our plans for the upcoming week. As we were talking, I noticed a handsome young man waiting on a table not far from where we were seated. I was almost distracted by his smile. He had the prettiest smile that I had ever seen. He wore a blue dress shirt, with dark trousers. He was sporting the same fade haircut that Keno wore. He also had the same gleam in his eyes that Keno had when I first met him. I noticed that he had been watching me, and we had caught each other's eye several times. I felt the urgency to meet him up close and personal, so I decided to speak up.

"Sheba, do you see that guy over there?" I asked as I pointed over towards the kitchen area of the restaurant.

"Yes, why?" Sheba replied.

"I just have to meet him," I cheerfully shouted.

"Oh," Dora hastily interrupted, "that's Gary. He's a real

nice guy. A lot of girls out here like him, but he nah give dem no play."

"Tell him to come here," I desperately demanded. As Dora and Gary were walking over towards the table where Sheba and I were seated, I began to feel butterflies in my stomach. Although I was very nervous, I pretended that I was calm.

"Gary, I want you to meet Sabrina. Sabrina, this is Gary."

"Hi, Gary."

"Hello, Sabrina, pleased to meet you," he politely replied as he rubbed the side of his face. "Sabrina, come over here and sit with me for a minute," Gary demanded. "I want to talk with you." Gary swiftly led me to the other side of the room to a table that was far away from the front door of the restaurant. "So, Sabrina, how long have you been in Jamaica? Is this your first time here?"

"Well," I replied, "I have been here for a week. I came to visit the island with my best friend, over there," I replied as I pointed towards the direction of where Sheba and her Aunt Dora were comfortably seated. "This is my first time visiting the island."

"You look very nice, Sabrina. I was watching you since you came into the restaurant," Gary exclaimed in a loud but appealing Jamaican accent. "Sabrina, where are you staying, in town or in the country? If you didn't know, this side of town is called the country."

"We're staying at the Jamaica Inn, not too far from here. I guess you can say that we're staying in the country." We both laughed.

"Well, Sabrina, I live in the part of Jamaica that we call the country. I live on this side of town, not too far from here. How about if I stop by, maybe tomorrow after work, about six o'clock?"

"That would be great," I cheerfully replied. "When you

come to the hotel, just ask for Sabrina, Sabrina Matheson."

"Okay, I will see you tomorrow night. It was nice talking with you, Sabrina. I see the boss coming; I'd better be leaving." I was desperate to receive confirmation for Gary coming to visit me at the hotel tomorrow. I felt the urgency to question him.

"So, Gary, are you sure that you will come to visit me tomorrow?"

"Yeah, man, don't worry, be happy. I'm definitely coming to see you." Although we didn't exchange telephone numbers, for some reason I was satisfied with his promise. Gary was someone that I could fall in love with, I thought. I decided to crown him as my new king. The thought of him being my king was exciting. He was different. He spoke with an accent. He was gentle. He was Jamaican.

The evening that Gary had promised to meet me at the hotel finally arrived. Sheba and I were talking about our junior high school days, and eating a snack. Suddenly, there was a loud knock on the door.

"Who is it?" Sheba exclaimed.

"It's Gary," replied the individual at the door. Before Sheba could turn around, I was there, reaching for the doorknob, in order to let Gary in.

"Come in, have a seat, Gary," I demanded. Gary had on a colorful shirt, with a pair of white trousers. He had on an attractive cologne, which reminded me of Keno. He also had the gleam in his eyes, the same gleam that I noticed on the day that I met him. It was the same gleam that Keno had in his eyes. I was determined not to allow the reminders of Keno to prevent me from getting to know Gary. As Gary entered the room, Sheba pretended to make herself occupied with different books that she had in the drawer.

"So, hi Gary, you did keep your word about coming to visit

me."

"Yes," he exclaimed as he showed off his pearly white smile, "I told you that I would visit, and I kept my word."

Gary and I began to spend most of the time together during the last four days of our stay in Jamaica. We visited many of his relatives, went out to dinner, and visited the beach. It was finally time for Sheba and I to go back home. It was a bright, sunny Sunday morning when Gary met us at the airport in Montego Bay. He had expressed that he wanted to see us off to New York, and converse while we waited for our flight to leave the island.

"Sabrina," Gary politely asked, "how did you like your visit to Jamaica?"

"I loved it," I exclaimed in a loud voice, as if I were announcing it to the universe. "Like we discussed last evening, I'm going to come back in October to visit you."

"I would be looking forward to seeing you again, Sabrina." Spending time with Gary made me feel important again. He gave me all of the attention that I missed since breaking up with Keno.

"So you two love birds are going to see each other real soon, eh?" Sheba questioned in her famous motherly tone of voice.

"Yes," Gary replied, she's my special one. I'm looking forward to seeing her again."

Before we knew it, the time had come for us to board the airplane. Gary promised that he would call, and I did the same. Sheba and I could see Gary standing at the waving stand at the airport, as we sat waiting for our flight to leave the runway. As our flight ascended into the air, I began to feel as if I had accomplished something great. I had met someone who really cared about me, and enjoyed spending quality time with me. Gary made me feel special again. I was looking forward to seeing him again.

Two days had passed by since I came back home from Jamaica. It was a warm day in September. I had just began my senior year in college. I was getting ready for my two o'clock class, when the telephone rang.

"Hello."

"Hi, this is the New York telephone operator. I have a collect call from Gary; would you accept?"

"Yes, I will. Hello, hello," I exclaimed.

"Hi, Sabrina, this is Gary. How are you doing, my special one?"

"I'm fine; I miss you."

"I miss you too," Gary replied.

"I'm preparing to go to my class. Remember, I told you that I would be graduating from college in May, right?"

"Yes, Sabrina, I remember you telling me, and I did promise you that I'd be there. My father filed for me to come to Canada to live with him. He told me that the paperwork should be ready by sometime in April."

"That's good. I would love to have you present. It would make me so happy."

"Sabrina, when I come up there, I'm going to take good care of you. I will pay the rent, and treat you really nice." Gary's words made me feel like I could conquer the world. His words were the temporary relief for the pain that I had felt as a result of Keno and I breaking up.

"So, Gary, I'm on my way out; you can call me later on." As I proceeded to grab my books, the phone rang again. It was my father, Mr. Barnes. I had not spoken to him about the vacation yet. I did speak to my mother, and I told her about my meeting Gary. Surprisingly, she had no opinion at all concerning Gary, not to mention his collect calls being billed to her phone. I wasn't certain of my father's reaction to my telling him about Gary, but it was worth a shot.

"Hello, Sabrina, how are you? I figured that I'd give you a few days to settle in before I called you in order to ask about your getaway to Jamaica. So, how was your trip?"

"It was very nice," I reluctantly replied. "I met most of Sheba's family. They were really nice. We went to the beach, and shopping. We had a nice time."

"So who's this guy Larry or something, that you met in Jamaica? Your mom told me earlier when I had called for you."

"Oh, Gary. He's a nice guy that I met."

"Sabrina, let me tell you something. I did not send you to Jamaica to bring back a souvenir that could cost you your life."

"Oh, no Dad, it's not that serious." My father was unstoppable with his words. He was determined to get his point across.

"Sabrina, you done went to the bottom of the barrel. I mean, if you want a husband you could find one from America. Don't make me feel like I've made a mistake, when I thought that I was helping you by sending you on vacation," he pleaded. It was obvious that he and my mother talked about the situation. I figured that I would just play it cool.

"No, Dad, don't worry, he's just a friend."

"Okay, I'm just letting you know, as a man, you need to take your time. Don't go having kids, because I'm telling you, this man that you met does not want any responsibilities." My father was talking like he actually knew Gary.

Gary and I wrote many letters, and sent cards with pictures to each other. We spoke to each other every day. Gary had sent me a nice pair of gold earrings in the mail. I went to visit him in Jamaica during the months of October and November. We spent intimate times together, and enjoyed evenings out on the town. I began to feel like a brand new person. I was in love with Gary. He began to become the center of my life. When I learned that Keno got married to someone else, it did not bother me. I began to mentally paint pictures of Gary in the compartments of my mind. Gary was constantly assuring me that he would be present at my graduation in May.

One day, I decided to go shopping at the Big Apple Bazaar in order to pick out a bracelet and a few shirts for Gary. On my way, north of the Bazaar, I walked past a booth. I felt as if a magnet pulled me back. I looked up and noticed a sign which read "Spiritual Readings by Mrs. Mary." I was always told as a child that one should stay away from people who perform readings. Our family Pentecostal religion preached against getting involved with such influences. I was very curious. I began to feel helpless. I quickly walked into the booth and noticed a woman sitting in a bamboo-wicker chair. She appeared to be a charming, young, pale-faced woman with long black hair. Her eyes gleamed with the glow of deep green candles. The aroma of the booth reminded me of freshly-picked rose petals. Her entire presence was almost magical. She must have known that I was new to this world. As I reached out my hand and curiously touched one of the crystals that were placed on the table nearby where she was sitting, she began to lure me into her trap. It was as if the predator had mystically mastered the prey.

"Hello, sweetie, have a seat," she slyly commanded, "you need a reading."

"What does that mean," I replied in a soft voice.

"You need me to tell you your future. There is a lot of evil around you." After that statement, I was convinced that she was telling the truth.

"How much do you charge?"

"Only twenty-five dollars." I felt as if I were being intimidated. I almost felt helpless. I reached into my wallet and handed her the twenty-five dollars.

"Okay," she stated as she pulled out a deck of cards from the drawer. As she was shuffling the cards, I began to notice strange looking cards. I have never seen any cards like such in my life. There were cards with the face of a devil, some cards with angels, and many other distinctive-looking cards.

"Pick seven," she stated as she mysteriously glanced into my eyes. "Wow, who's the guy that you just met? I see a new relationship. Is he overseas?"

"Yes," I replied.

"He's very sick," she yelled as she added seven more cards to the pile of cards that were already on the table. "It looks like somebody gave him poison to drink which caused him to have problems with his stomach. Looks like a lady did it. Many women like him. She wants to be his wife. She tried to trap him. Something's going on with his visa. Is he trying to get here?"

"Yes," I replied, "his father filed for him. He's just waiting to hear from the embassy." During the entire time sitting there listening to her, I was literally being spooked trying to figure out how she knew this information.

"What's your name, sweetie?" she asked in a luring monotone voice.

"Sabrina."

"Okay, Sabrina, I can help you. I can help you get Gary here to America faster. I can also help you keep Gary to yourself. I will also help him with his stomach problem."

I was so elated. This woman was telling me exactly what I wanted to hear. She made my day.

"Sabrina, I will start all of the work for two hundred dollars. You can give me one hundred now, and come back next Sunday with the balance. Sabrina, take this red candle. I want you to write your name one time on it, and Gary's name next to yours. Light the candle for fifteen minutes for five nights." I reached into my wallet and quickly handed her five twenty dollar bills. She aggressively began to explain the spiritual plans that she had for Gary.

"Thank you, Mrs. Mary," I exclaimed. I started to believe that Mrs. Mary was my best friend. I trusted her. I could not wait to leave the Big Apple Bazaar so that I could call Gary and tell him what the Tarot card reader told me. Was Gary really a sick man? Were there really that many women that wanted his attention? Could she really help me get him into the country quicker, so that he would be at my graduation? I had to believe her. She was the only one that was helping me to live my fantasy about being together with Gary. I was convinced that once I burned the red candle that she gave me, Gary would not be attracted to the women in Jamaica who wanted his attention. The money that I gave her was nothing compared to what could happen if I did not cooperate with her. I quickly returned to the counter and paid for the bracelet, shirts and cologne that I picked out for Gary. I could not wait to contact him.

When I reached home, I could not wait to drop the packages. I rushed over to the telephone, and dialed Gary's number.

"Gary, guess what? While I was out shopping for a few things for you, I went to a Tarot card reader." Gary was silent. "She told me that somebody gave you poison to drink and that as a result, you are having a lot of problems with your stomach. She also told me that she could help the process of your visa for Canada come through quicker. She told me that she could help you with your stomach too." I refused to tell him about the women who wanted to be his wife. I would handle that separately.

"Wow, Sabrina, who is this woman? She's absolutely

correct. I have been having a lot of problems with my stomach. I've been sick for a while, but I did not want to tell you. I even threw up on several occasions while you were down here, but I did not tell you. I have been to many doctors, but they all tell me that there's nothing wrong. I even let them put the tube down into my stomach, but they found nothing. My sister even took my jacket to a reader here in Jamaica, and they told her the same thing."

"Oh, my goodness, Gary." I instantly felt the obligation to help him get well. "Don't worry, Mrs. Mary guaranteed me that she would help you. She also guaranteed me that she would speed up the process of you getting your visa to Canada. Just think about it, Gary, you coming to America, and we'll be together. You will also get help with your stomach. Mrs. Mary told me to come back on Sunday so that I could get a candle to burn so that your visa papers would be processed faster. She is also giving me a candle and bath so that your stomach would feel better. She told me that I have to give her some more money so that she could start the work. Mrs. Mary said that when you come to America she will cure your stomach condition."

"Oh, Sabrina, you really are my special one. I love you."

"I love you too, Gary."

"Oh, Sabrina, my special one, when I move to Canada, I want you to come visit me at my father's house, okay?"

"No problem." We both laughed. Shortly after we spoke, I went to the post office and mailed Gary his bracelet, shirts, and cologne. I was happy again. Gary needed me.

I went back to the Big Apple Bazaar in order to see Mrs. Mary. She appeared very happy to see me.

"Hi, Sabrina," she stated as she sipped on a tall glass of water.

"Hi, Mrs. Mary. I came to drop off the hundred dollars to

contribute to the work that you are doing for Gary."

"Sabrina, I went to the gods last night and they told me that I have to charge you one thousand dollars for the work that I need to do for you. I will take the hundred, but you will owe me a balance of nine hundred." I was guessing that the hundred dollars that I gave her last week was just a bonus.

"Well, Mrs. Mary, I was not expecting to spend so much money today. I'm still a student and I don't have much cash around."

"Well," she angrily replied, "can't you go to your credit cards, borrow it, or apply for a loan?" Mrs. Mary obviously wasn't concerned about how I got the money, she just wanted it. Her very presence intimidated me. Who were the "gods" that she spoke about? The mystery in her words made me anxious and fearful. I would find the money out of fear and intimidation.

"Okay, Mrs. Mary, I will be back tomorrow with the balance." The strange look in her eyes was a warning to me, but I had no other option but to bring her the money. I called Sheba and five other people that I had not spoken to in months, in order to borrow the money that I needed for Mrs. Mary. It was a stressful task, but I finally raised the money. I went back to Mrs. Mary the following week and gave her the nine hundred dollars.

"Don't worry, Sabrina, I'm going to help you. Gary will be here in no time. Do you trust me?" she asked in a sly, but convincing tone of voice.

"Yes, I do."

"Here, Sabrina, take these crystals home with you and this incense cone. Put the crystals under the pillow before you pray, and light the cone incense."

"Thank you, Mrs. Mary, I will let you know when Gary comes to the States."

"Be sure to bring him here, so that I can finish helping him. Gary will call you sometime in April and will tell you that he's on his way to Canada to live; trust me, Sabrina."

During the month of March, Gary and I spoke on the phone, and wrote letters to each other more than ever. One day, during the first week of April, Gary telephoned me.

"Sabrina, guess what, my visa is ready. I will be moving to Canada next week."

"That is wonderful. See, Gary, Mrs. Mary is really doing a great job helping us." "The only problem that I'm having is with my stomach," replied Gary.

"Don't worry, Gary, you will be with me in New York soon. She will help you. I already paid for the work."

"Sabrina, I want to see you. Here's the information where my father lives. I would like you to meet me there in Canada."

"That would be great." Gary gave me the information. I would work out my schedule, even if I were to meet him for only three days.

I booked a round trip flight to Ontario, Canada. The flight to Canada was comfortable and quick. After the flight landed, I looked for a taxi. As one approached I got into the back seat.

"Hello, I would like to go to 122 Sandpipe Road." As the taxi drove up to the house, I noticed Gary and a man who appeared quite older than him standing on the porch. They were expecting me and waiting for my arrival.

As I stepped out of the taxi, Gary ran up to the car and grabbed my luggage out of the trunk.

"Hello, Sabrina," he shouted, as I paid the driver the fare for my ride. "This is my father, Bob. Bob, this is my girlfriend, Sabrina from New York."

"Hi, Sabrina," stated his father as he abruptly shook my hand. "Come inside and make yourself comfortable, Sabrina."

As I stepped into the house, I noticed a lot of plants placed against the entire back wall of the living room. The furniture in the living room reminded me of a royal palace. The aroma of freshly lit incense intensely overpowered the perfume that I was wearing. On that evening Gary and I enjoyed a well-prepared Jamaican dinner at his father's home. Three days had already passed by. Gary and I enjoyed the sights of Toronto, Canada. We spent a lot of time dancing at the clubs, going to the movies, and bowling.

On one evening before going to bed, Gary asked me to come into the basement in order to talk to him. I found that to be quite odd, since we had never spent time together in that area of the house since I'd been visiting.

"Sabrina, how are you enjoying yourself so far?" Gary asked.

"Fine, I really like it here. It's much different from New York."

All of a sudden, almost out of the blue sky, Gary punched me in the side of my face.

"Why did you do that," I angrily exclaimed. "Get away from me," I shouted as I ran upstairs.

"What happened?" exclaimed Gary's father Bob.

"Gary just threw a punch in my face, for no reason." As I finished my sentence, Gary ran upstairs after me.

"I'm sorry Sabrina, please forgive me. I don't know what happened to me." Although I was still in a state of shock, trying to figure out why Gary struck me, I forgave him.

It was finally time for me to go back home to New York. Gary arranged my transportation to the airport. The flight home was very quick and comfortable.

I had no problem getting back into the swing of going to my classes. Besides, the special month was quickly approaching. I was looking forward to graduating in May, and of course having Gary here in town.

It was a cool, breezy day in the beginning of the month of May when Gary telephoned me with good news. "Hi, Sabrina, my special one, how are you today?"

"I'm better now that I'm hearing your voice."

"I wanted you to know that I will be in New York to visit you in two weeks. Isn't it great? I will be able to come to your graduation, just like I promised you. As long as I have my visa, I can travel to New York." I was excited, but at the same time speechless.

The day that Gary came to New York finally approached. I had made arrangements to pick Gary up from the airport in Newark, New Jersey. As Gary entered into the waiting area of the Air Canada flights, I greeted him with a hug. "Hi, Gary," I exclaimed. "It's a pleasure finally meeting with you on American soil." We both laughed, as Gary kissed me on the cheek.

I enjoyed giving Gary a tour of New York and pointing out famous landmarks during our cab ride back to Staten Island. We finally got back to my apartment. When Gary had previously told me that he was coming to New York, I had made arrangements to rent a beautiful studio apartment. I had also landed an evening job counseling troubled teens at the local group home, which paid my bills and allowed me to enjoy extra leisure activities.

"So, Sabrina, this is a very nice apartment."

"Thanks, Gary, you can just put your suitcase down over there," I stated as I pointed to the oversized closet located near the front door. Gary seemed a little suspicious and almost cynical as he sat at the kitchen table. He began making facial gestures, as if he had a hidden agenda regarding something or someone. I didn't make a big deal about it. Although he was a stranger, I made up my mind that I would treat him as if I'd known him for years. Gary and I spent a lot of time together going to the movies, and meeting up with some of my family and old acquaintances.

Gary kept his word. On May 23rd, he attended my graduation from Wagner College. It was a very exciting day.

A week following my graduation, it was time for Gary to go back to Canada. "Well, Sabrina, it's time for me to go back home the day after tomorrow." All of a sudden, I began to feel as if I had just lost my best friend. I was not satisfied with hearing what Gary was saying. Gary was the only person that I had to keep me company. I was determined to make him an offer that he could not refuse.

"Gary," I exclaimed, "we could get married, so that you would not have to go back home. If we get married, the Immigration Department will not harass you about going back to Canada."

All of a sudden, Gary's face lit up like a light bulb. "Oh, Sabrina," Gary shouted, "that would be a great idea."

"Gary, we can go down to the Justice of the Peace, and they will perform the ceremony. I will ask my mother and my aunt to be witnesses. We'll go down there in two days, in order to get the information."

"Sabrina, what about us meeting with Mrs. Mary, the reader? Remember, you said that she would help me with my stomach?"

"Oh, yeah," I casually replied. I almost forgot. As a matter of fact, let us go down to the Big Apple Bazaar today in order to meet her." I called a taxi to take us to meet Mrs. Mary.

As we got out of the taxi, Gary put his hand on his stomach and made gestures, as if he were attempting to vomit. "Excuse me, Sabrina, I'm very sorry. My stomach is in a lot of pain."

"Don't worry," I replied, "we're going inside to see Mrs. Mary, who can help you."

As we approached the booth where Mrs. Mary was seated,

I noticed several statues of saints in the front. It was almost as if they were greeting us. There was a statue of Mary, Michael the Archangel, and others that I've never seen before. As I pulled the curtain back, in anticipation of seeing Mrs. Mary, she was seated in her royal seat, surrounded by white candles. The incense burned with a strong scent of sweet candy. Mrs. Mary appeared as if she were expecting our visit. Her mystical eyes gave me a chill as she greeted me. "Hi, Sabrina, I was wondering when you were going to bring him to me."

As Gary and I sat in the two chairs positioned directly in front of where she was seated, I proceeded to introduce her to Gary. "Mrs. Mary, this is Gary, from Jamaica."

"Hi, Gary, it's a pleasure to meet you," she stated as she glanced over to the window. "So, Gary, I have been helping Sabrina with your visa. It's because of me that you were able to get to America so quickly. I have also been praying to the gods for you, concerning the issue with your stomach. You know that someone—a lady—gave you something to drink. It should have killed you by now, but I've been doing extra prayers for you, which saved you. Now," stated Mrs. Mary as she turned over seven cards from a deck of cards, "I'm looking into your belly. It is very black. I can get it out, but the gods are telling me that it's going to cost you five thousand U.S. dollars. They're telling me that I have to go to the graveyard to do the work."

I could not believe what I was hearing. Gary was reacting like he was used to receiving predictions regarding his life. This type of information was all new to me. Mrs. Mary quoted five thousand dollars as if it were one dollar. I was eager to interject but before I could, Gary interrupted.

"I'm so happy, Mrs. Mary," Gary shouted in his country Jamaican accent. "When Sabrina told me that you told her the condition about my stomach, I couldn't believe it. It was as if I were dreaming. I went everywhere in Jamaica for help, and spent so much money, and nobody could help me."

"Well, you'd better be thankful for me," she exclaimed. "I am the one who could take this spell off of you. Somebody did witchcraft to you—an evil spell. I am the one who will reverse it with my witchcraft. I'm not like these other spiritual people that you see around. I am an Israelite," Mrs. Mary exclaimed, as she cast her mystical eyes on the both of us. "You just bring me at least three thousand dollars so that I can start the work," she demanded. Both Gary and I thanked her for her help. "Before you go, take these candles, one white you burn at night-time, and the red one, burn during the day for good luck. Gary, you eat these peanuts. Take about a handful of these each morning for five days. It will help you with the gas and bloating that you are experiencing."

As we were walking out of the Bazaar Gary exclaimed, "How did she know that I had gas and bloating? I never told her." We both laughed. I began to feel as if finally, my life was back on track. I was getting married, and we had some-body who was helping us with Gary's problem. We weren't worried about raising the money for Mrs. Mary.

Two days later we went to Borough Hall. We obtained all of the information. I decided to pay the fee, and get our marriage over with. I called my mother and told her the good news. "Hi, Mom, Gary and I are down here at Borough Hall. We need a witness, because we are going to get married right away."

"Sabrina, I know that at the graduation you were briefly speaking about the possibility, but are you sure that this is what you want to do?"

"Yes," I replied.

"Okay, well, if this is that you want, your Aunt Debbie and I will meet you both down at Borough Hall in order to be witnesses."

My mother and aunt met Gary and I at Borough Hall. Gary and I were finally married. Gary's family in Canada were not too happy about him not coming back to Canada, but we didn't care. I introduced Gary to my landlord, who was a director for a large insurance agency in New York City. He was able to introduce us to an immigration lawyer who handled Gary's green card paperwork. My landlord appointed Gary with a full time position working in the insurance office with overtime, paid vacation, and medical benefits. Gary didn't believe it, but he was blessed.

It was time for me to apply for my new job with the local utility company. We finally saved up two thousand dollars, when we decided to go visit Mrs. Mary. Mrs. Mary had the usual mystical look on her face. "Oh, come in, sit down," she stated in a tone of victory.

"We have so much to tell you," I exclaimed. "Gary and I got married, and he got a really great job. I'm about to apply for the job that the college offered me."

"Well," replied Mrs. Mary, "I hope that you both realize that it is because of me. I am the one that is helping the both of you," she angrily stated. "I'm doing all of this work, and I'm not getting any money from you."

"Mrs. Mary, we have two thousand dollars of the money that you requested. If you can help us, we can pay the balance off over time."

"This is not a bank," she hastily replied, "but you both are young, and I will work with you. Sabrina, by the way, you're pregnant. We better get Gary healed right away. You don't want the baby to be born with this bad luck that Gary has."

By now, I was more than afraid. I was terrified. I quickly gave Mrs. Mary the two thousand dollars, which were all hundred dollar bills. We all went into the back of the area where Mrs. Mary was practicing her magic. She held a jar of warm water that was sealed.

"Gary, now you put your hand on top of my hand as we shake this water up and down." They both had their hands on the jar, shaking it up and down. "Harder, shake the jar harder," she shouted as Gary desperately followed her command. Finally, after about forty desperate shakes of the jar of water, a huge, thick black smog entered into the jar. It was almost as if someone poured tar into the water.

"Wow," we all exclaimed.

"This black smog that you see in the jar of water is what was inside of your stomach. How do you feel?"

"I feel much better, Mrs. Mary. Oh, thank you, you healed me. I don't feel the pain that was in my stomach."

"You are welcome," replied Mrs. Mary. "Just don't forget that I'm the one who is helping you. Make sure that you come back with the balance of three thousand dollars, so that the bad luck won't come back. Oh, and Sabrina, take this cone of incense and candle and light the both of them together for good luck with your job."

We were both so happy. A week later I found out that I was pregnant. Gary didn't seem so happy about it, but he was a very good pretender. Gary and I decided that Mrs. Mary was overcharging us, and that we would find someone else to help us. Although I was pregnant, I was able to gain a very good paying job with the local utility company.

Over the next three weeks, Gary's demeanor changed. He became very controlling, and at times physically abusive. It did not matter to him that I was pregnant with his child. He was becoming more and more unreasonable as the days went by. I was spending more time arguing and fighting with Gary than anything else. Gary began to isolate me from my family, and the few associates that I had, including my best friend

Sheba.

One day, while Gary was at work during the evening, the phone rang.

"Hello."

"Hi, Sabrina, this is your father. Where have you been? What the heck is going on?"

"Well, Dad, the guy from Jamaica came here from Canada to visit, and we got married." There was brief silence before Mr. Barnes became hysterical.

"What, are you kidding me? Sabrina, you just graduated from college. What's wrong with you? You went to the bottom of the barrel with this one." Before I was able to say one word, Mr. Barnes hung up the phone.

When Gary came home from work, we agreed that we were both being spiritually fixed by Mrs. Mary, and that we would find a witch from Brooklyn to help us. I was already six months pregnant with Gary Junior. By this time we had our own vehicle. We decided to drive around Brooklyn in search of our new spiritual reader. Finally, we passed a huge building which had a sign which read "Readings by Ms. Zuma." Wow, I thought, she must be really good. We parked the vehicle in front of the shop. As we entered into the storefront, there was religious music playing, something about "Jesus will help you" and "Satan, your kingdom must come down." The store smelled like a combination of freshly scented oils. On one side of the wall there were eight ounce candles arranged by colors in glass holders. I noticed many statues of saints on display, for sale. As we approached the counter, a girl who appeared to be about fifteen years old offered to assist us.

"May I help you?"

"Yes," I replied, "we would like to speak with the reader."

"Oh, very good, she's an excellent reader, and she helps a lot of people. She is very busy right now, but if you like, you may wait."

"How much does she charge for a reading?"

"Oh, only thirty dollars."

"Okay, we'll wait."

There were many people waiting to see this so-called Ms. Zuma. As we were waiting to see her, a burst of smoke-filled incense illuminated the entire room. Gary and I began to cough. Finally, after waiting for about one hour, a short woman with a scarf tied backwards on her head appeared from behind a shrine of beads. She had on dark clothes, and had a dark complexion. She spoke with a West Indian accent. It was evident that she had her surroundings under complete control. She spoke with authority, walked with authority, and made gestures with authority. It was obvious that the girl in the front who offered to assist us feared her.

"Who's next?" the woman asked as she placed a newly-lit purple candle on the countertop.

"We are," I anxiously shouted.

As she led us into the back of the store, I began to feel spooked. There was a black chicken running around the area. There were many candles lit on the countertop. There was a deck of cards sitting on the table with a monkey's paw on display.

"So, how may I help you?" she asked in a monotone voice.

I was anxious to give her our report. "We are here because we went to a reader over in Staten Island. She said that we had to pay her five thousand U.S. dollars for helping my husband with his stomach. We gave her two thousand dollars, but we don't think that we should pay the rest. It's too much money. We also have been fighting a whole lot."

"Pick ten cards," she stated as she finished shuffling the deck of cards that was on the table. As I handed her the ten cards, she flipped them over, and frowned. "Wow, I see that this woman is robbing you. She can't help you. She's upset because she feels that you owe her money. I can help you. First, I need you to buy five different statues of saints. You have to have them in your home in order to receive power."

I didn't mind, since Gary and I had planned on moving to a larger apartment during the next month. I would have more room.

"I also need you to buy two black pull-out candles. We have to reverse the curse that the reader that you went to before put on you both. I want you to write her name on the candle seven times. You will tell the girl up front to give you some destruction oil and power oil. You must burn these candles for fifteen minutes, twice a day. Also, you both need to take cleansing baths. You still have time. Just start off by doing this first. You can leave me two hundred dollars, and we'll take it one day at a time. Come see me in about two weeks."

I handed her the money, and proceeded to purchase the candles, oils, and five statues of saints. When we arrived at our new apartment, I put the saints on display. Every morning and evening we prayed to the saints for direction and comfort. We also lit the candles as directed.

Gary Jr. was finally born. Gary and I began to fight every day. Gary became more verbally and physically abusive. It seemed like the more I prayed to the saints about my issues, the worse the problems became. The police came to the house many times, as a result of Gary's abusive behavior. I never had the courage to have him arrested for his actions. Gary and I continued our rituals for about a year. We prayed often to the statues, and lighted our candles. I became pregnant again, and gave birth to Rebecca.

The violence became very intense between Gary and me. I found myself paying all of the bills, even though Gary worked. One day, Gary and I decided that we needed to go back in order to visit Ms. Zuma for guidance. We brought Gary Jr. and Rebecca to my mother's house for the day.

When we arrived at Ms. Zuma's storefront, she was standing outside, as if she were expecting our arrival. "Come in, I was waiting for you to come back," she stated as she held the door open for us. As she led us to the rear of the storefront, a black rooster ran towards us. "Don't panic," she demanded. "This is what you need in your house for protection." As we sat down, Ms. Zuma began to write on a piece of paper. "I've been thinking about the both of you. I want to perform a total cleansing for you and your family. It will cost you two thousand dollars."

As I attempted to speak, Gary abruptly interrupted me, and said, "No problem. I will bring you the money next week."

I found that to be quite strange because next week was a major holiday. We needed the money to buy food.

"Ms. Zuma, why can't you do it this week?" questioned Gary.

"I can only do it on Saturday. You both come along with your two children. Come when the store is closed. I think that it would be fine if you came here around eight o'clock in the night. Before you come, I need you to stop off at the live poultry store and purchase two live chickens, one male and one female. Also, go to the pet store and bring me a brown male rabbit. I need these for sacrifices," Ms. Zuma exclaimed. Gary and I proceeded to leave the shop.

During the week leading up to our spiritual cleansing, Gary and I prayed diligently to the saints. A voice came to me, and told me to set up an altar with candy, donuts, red wine, and bread. I don't know who the voice represented, but I obeyed. I was also instructed to put flowers on the altar, and light a green candle for money, and a red candle for love. Each day that I checked the altar it appeared as if the wine was slowly disappearing as if someone were drinking it. The candy and bread on the altar was distributed among Gary, myself, and the children. By the time we ate the pastries, it appeared as if something or someone had sapped the flavor from everything that was on the altar. The candles on the altar burned with passion. The Caridad statue that I prayed to appeared to be crying. It was as if she felt the sudden terror that we would soon experience.

Saturday quickly arrived. Before we left in order to see Ms. Zuma, I replaced the wine, bread, and pastries on the altar. I also lit a white candle for clearance, as instructed by the voice in my head. On our way to Zuma's shop, we stopped off at the pet shop, and bought a brown rabbit. We also stopped at the live poultry shop, and bought one male chicken and one female chicken.

When we arrived at Zuma's shop, she demanded that we all take off our clothes. Gary, the two children and I stood up naked in a tub of water that she prepared for us. "You all need thorough cleansing. This whole family is cursed. I'm going to mix a bath for all of you. Once I'm finished, I have to pour it over your head. This will be the beginning of the cleansing. Gary," she demanded, "give me the two thousand dollars."

After Gary handed her the money, which was twenty one hundred dollar bills, she threw it on the floor, next to the rabbit that we bought. The bath that she was mixing smelled very sweet. Gary Jr. and Rebecca began to cry. Once she finished mixing the bath, she poured the liquid over all of our heads. The bath that she gave us lasted for about one hour. Zuma gave us each a white sheet to wrap around our bodies. Zuma led us all up to the front of the store. She began chanting. She proceeded to light a cigar, and smoke it. Zuma commanded us all to stand up in the middle of the room. Zuma began to surround us in a circle, using white chalk. She also drew symbols of the cross and unfamiliar symbols. She began to light tall white candles, and placed them in the circle with us. Zuma put on some music, which resembled African tribal music. Zuma fell into a trance, and picked up a bottle of vodka, and began spitting the vodka onto the light of the candles. She began to foam at the mouth. Zuma proceeded to light two additional candles. These two were red.

Zuma grabbed the first chicken out of the bag. It was as if the chicken knew that her life was being sacrificed for something. Zuma gave me the female chicken and gave Gary the male chicken. Zuma commanded me, first to cut off the neck of the female chicken. Zuma handed me the knife as she rang the large bell that she held in her hand.

"Sabrina, cut the neck." I was totally in shock, but I knew that this had to be done. I grabbed the knife into my hand and began to aggressively cut the neck of the chicken. The blood began to quickly drip out of the chicken's neck, when Zuma yelled, "Drop the blood over the candles. Drop the blood over the candles." I dripped the blood from the chicken's neck onto the candles, and threw the head onto the candle and the body remained moving on the floor. Gary proceeded to do the same thing that I did, using the male chicken. After Gary finished, Zuma took the chickens and began to rub both chickens on each of us as she chanted in an unfamiliar voice. Gary Jr. and Rebecca began to scream. After the ritual was over, Zuma rushed to put the bloody candles and dead chickens into a bag.

"Sabrina and Gary, this bag contains the dead chickens. On your way home, drop the dead chickens at any busy intersection. Do not let anyone see you. You must hurry. Also, write what you desire for your enemies on this piece of parchment paper."

After we wrote our wish, we gave Zuma the two pieces of paper. Gary and I both watched Zuma as she aggressively stuffed the two pieces of parchment paper into the anus of the rabbit. I found it to be quite cruel, but Ms. Zuma demanded that this needed to be done. "I am going to take this rabbit with me to the cemetery," she stated. "I have a lot of work to do."

Gary and I drove off, looking for a busy intersection to throw the bags into. Finally, we approached a busy intersection. I rolled the window down on the passenger side where I was sitting.

"Now drop it," yelled Gary. I quickly dropped the bag, hoping that nobody would see me. I was happy that nobody actually saw me dropping the bag of dead chickens.

Zuma, Gary and I performed many rituals also with pigeons, in order to gain spiritual power. We practiced for at least three years. Gary and I visited Ms. Zuma every week. I found myself spending two hundred dollars or more each week buying candles, incense, and oils in order to protect myself from my enemies.

Gary and I began to have even more fights and arguments. Gary managed to cut himself with a piece of glass, call the police and claim that I assaulted him. Of course, they arrested me. I was the individual being abused, but the abuser was able to set me up. After three days, I was released on my own recognizance. Is this what I graduated from college for? I slowly began to feel as if my self-esteem was going lower and lower as the days moved on. I found it difficult to keep steady employment, and maintain motherhood, due to the stress that I was experiencing.

I remember Ms. Zuma telling me that I had the ability to become a spiritual reader. I decided to open my own business. I made spiritual baths for my clients, and gave them spiritual readings and candles for a fee.

Gary and I began to have more and more conflict. I began

to feel out of control. I turned to alcohol in order to alleviate the stress. Many nights I made it home, not knowing how I made it. My mother stepped in, and helped me raise my two children. Gary was still around arguing with me, and physically abusing me. Drinking alcohol began to be part of my daily ritual. It got to the point where I could not read a tarot card without taking a drink. I was under so much stress.

One day a woman from the local church knocked on the door. "Hello," she yelled, "is anyone here?" I abruptly opened the door, and was surprised to see Sister Creston and Sister Diaz. "Sabrina, I was praying to the Lord about you and I didn't like what he showed me. Are you in need of help? We haven't seen you in church for a long time." As Sister Creston finished her sentence, she glanced around the living room and said, "In the name of Jesus, I cast down these idols." Sister Creston and Sister Diaz began to tear down my altar and removed all of my statues from the house.

I began to cry and fell on my knees. "Help, I need help, they're going to get me," I screamed.

Sister Creston and Sister Diaz began praying and speaking in a foreign tongue. After the two sisters finished praying for me, they decided to talk to me. "Sabrina, I know that you grew up in the church, but something happened. If you want to be saved, repeat the sinner's prayer." Gary wasn't home, so I felt safe enough to speak.

"Sabrina, repeat after me. Dear Jesus, I admit that I am a sinner. Please forgive me for my sins. I believe that you died on the cross for the remission of my sins." I excitedly repeated the sinner's prayer.

"Now," exclaimed Sister Diaz, "you have been forgiven. We will be praying for you," she stated as Sister Creston lifted the heavy bag containing the idols. "Try to make your way to church. Remember, Jesus loves you, and so do I." As I closed the door, I felt a sense of peace. The apartment appeared strange without all of my statues and my altar present.

I began to feel nervous, as if someone were always watching me. I was afraid to stay home alone, when Gary left the apartment in order to go to work. I found no peace at home, so I felt the need to run. I ran to the bars looking for peace. I slowly began to lose everything. All of my clothes were slowly disappearing. Gary went into a rage and cut up most of my clothes with a knife. I owned one pair of shoes and one bra. All of my jewelry was gone. All of my friends were gone. Most of my family turned their backs on me. My enemies began to get the best of me. My husband Gary became even more abusive. My best friend Sheba ran away from me, as if I had a terrible contagious disease. It was difficult to sleep at night. Whenever I tried to go to sleep at night, it felt as if someone, or something, were having sexual intercourse with me, but nobody was there. I tried to comfort myself with alcohol. I began to feel as if I were hallucinating. I often felt as if someone were holding me down in my sleep, whenever I did go to sleep. I was tired all the time. My eyes had the appearance of constant bulging from my face, as if someone were chocking me. At times I would stay in my bed for weeks at a time. There were also times when I closed my eyes, that I literally saw dark-figured men wearing black hoods digging graves at a graveyard scene.

In the midst of my spiritual sickness, I managed to get an order of protection from Gary, which prevented him from coming back into the house. Since I was not working at the time, I was forced to apply for public assistance. This was the first time in my life that I ever had to do this. I was very depressed, and desperate for a breakthrough. I was treated as if I had no education or employment history. I was forced to work at job locations where I was overqualified and underpaid.

I was the very song of the drunkards. I dreaded going to the mall, because it was painful for me to see all of the pretty colors printed on the dresses and blouses. Besides, I had no money. I was at the lowest point of my life. I was slowly beginning to lose my memory. I could not remember major events of high school, nor college years. My mind had regressed to the mind of a seventeen year old girl. I became insecure about everything concerning myself and my future.

During my battle to stay alive, my mother agreed to allow Rebecca to stay with her. Gary Jr. stayed with me, while I tried to avoid the fiery flames from the burning missiles that were slowly destroying my life. The rent was past due, and it was beginning to become difficult to buy food and clothes for Gary Jr. and me. The marshal was scheduled to come in at any time in order to evict us.

One Monday evening I was relaxing in my apartment. Gary Jr. had spent the night at his best friend Ricky's house. I was feeling a little depressed at the time, and began drinking some wine. By the time I had finished, I began to feel even more depressed, and wondered why all of these things were happening to me. The pressure of being a single parent, with few resources or friends, began to overwhelm me. The voices in my head, telling me to come back to the readers for guidance, made me nervous.

Although I had refused to continue to work in the kingdom of Satan, I was still being harassed by the demons. All of the areas of my life became engulfed with a fire of hopelessness, which refused to release me. The saints from the church where I was baptized when I was a teen-ager never came and asked if I needed anything, or if I wanted them to pray for me. The more that I became engulfed in this dangerous fire, the more distant the saints became. It was as if they already declared me as being non-existent. Many days passed by. I felt as if I were existing, but I was not living my life. I was tired of running out of my apartment. I was tired of running out into nothingness. I was tired of running into the bars, searching for freedom. I was tired of not having any money. I was tired of existing.

One evening I was sitting in my empty apartment all alone. There were two twin beds, one for myself and one for Gary Jr. The small amount of belongings that Gary Jr. and I had were stored all around the room in thick, black trash bags. I decided that the bottle of wine that I had in my presence was my best friend. It was there when I needed it. It made me comfortable when I was feeling uneasy and anxious. Anything that I said, it agreed. As I poured the fifth glass of wine, I heard a voice. The voice said, "Go for a walk into the mall across the street. There is a man that you will meet who can help you." I didn't recognize the voice, but I was willing to take a chance and obey. I was desperate to find help. I was desperate to get out of the fire.

As I walked downstairs, already feeling tipsy from the wine that I was drinking previously, I managed to avoid tripping. I entered into the mall with great expectations. Who could this man be? Is there really someone who could really help me with all of these problems? I sat down in the main entrance and waited. Ironically, I met three men, one after the other, who gave me their phone numbers. I was not interested. I knew that not one of them were who I was sent to meet. After sitting down for about forty minutes, a young man walked up to me. He was accompanied by a young woman. She appeared to be overly-protective of him. I pretended as if I didn't see him, but the power of his presence forced me to make eye contact with him. It was him. This was the person that I was sent to meet. I was confident that he could help me. He walked closer to me, and the young lady stood behind him.

"Hi," I stated as he put the shopping bag down beside him. "I know you from the Stapleton area of Staten Island. I grew up there. You look familiar."

"Oh, yes," he replied. "I know you from Stapleton. I grew up there. What's your name?"

"Sabrina."

"Oh, yeah, Sabrina," he hastily replied. "Your face looks familiar, too." The woman who was walking with him realized that he was safe while speaking with me. She slowly walked away. He was a fair-skinned black man, and was built slightly. He had a gleam in his eyes which told me that he could help me. He was dressed in casual clothes, and had brown curly hair. "Here's my number; my name is Tanus."

"Okay," I replied. "This is my number," I stated as I handed him my home telephone number. "Call me. I have some things that I would like to share with you, Tanus."

"Okay, I will call you as soon as I get a chance, some time tonight."

"Okay, I will speak to you later."

I did not understand why this was all happening, but I was glad that I had someone to talk to. I was satisfied that I had met Tanus, and the purpose for my going to the mall was accomplished. As I entered my apartment, I felt a sigh of relief. It was not even fifteen minutes that I was home in my apartment when the phone rang.

"Hi, Sabrina, this is Tanus."

"Oh, hi, this is Sabrina." As I finished my sentence, I heard the voices in my head telling me to hang up the phone. They told me not to talk to Tanus. I abruptly hung up the phone. Two minutes later the phone rang again. I picked it up, and hung it up without saying a word. The phone rang again. This time I decided to answer the phone.

"Hello."

"Sabrina, it's Tanus. Why do you keep hanging up the phone on me every time that I call you?"

"Oh, I'm sorry," I exclaimed. "I think that I am having problems with my phone. I'm not hanging up on you." I was clearly telling a lie. There were no problems with my phone. I knew that Tanus could help me, and so did the demons.

"Sabrina, when I'm finished over here, I will call you." I began to wonder what this was all about. Even though I just met Tanus, I felt a connection. I believed that I could talk to him about everything that was happening to me, and around me. The next day Tanus called me. Since my phone hardly rang, I knew that it was him.

"Sabrina, I know that you told me that you have some things to talk to me about. Why don't you come over to my house and talk?"

"Okay, what's your address? I will take a cab."

"416 Jeroleum Place. I will wait for you," replied Tanus.

As the cab drove up to the white house, I began to feel nervous. I began to reassure myself that Tanus would understand me, and be able to help me. As I entered into the house, he pulled a chair out of the closet for me to sit on.

"So, Sabrina, what is on your mind?"

I began to feel as if I were in the psychologist's chair. I felt very comfortable. I was willing to take a chance, and "spill all of the beans" about my issues. "Well, Tanus, I'm going through a lot of problems. Something is happening to me. I lost everything, and my son and I are about to be evicted from our apartment. I don't have much money."

"I know that God can help you, Sabrina. It doesn't matter what you're going through, He will help you."

"I forgot to tell you that I used to be a reader. I was involved in rituals using pigeons and chickens as sacrifices," I confessed. "I used to read tarot cards and tell fortunes. It seems as if ever since I allowed two sisters from the church to tear down my altar and discard my idols, I've been experiencing more problems."

"Don't tell me," replied Tanus. "You gave up your service to the demons, and now they're harassing you. They took everything that you have, right?"

Wow, Tanus was speaking the same language. I felt as if he were the only individual who understood me. Tanus began to read the Bible to me. He took time out of his schedule in order to pray with me and study scripture from the Bible. On the nights that I could not sleep as a result of being harassed by the demons, Tanus stayed up on the phone with me praying and reading the Bible. There were times when Tanus would take me to the movies, and also out to eat dinner. I began to regain some of my memory that I lost. I began to learn more about my creator, Jesus Christ. The more time that I spent with Tanus reading the Bible and praying, I began to feel more alive. I started appreciating the colors of the rainbow. Going to the mall seeing colors on clothing didn't bother me anymore. I was spiritually waking up. Tanus was the first person that I saw when I awoke spiritually. We began to spend a lot of time together, enjoying each other's company. Over a period of twelve months, Tanus opened up my understanding of why I had to face the obstacles that I was up against. I began to have Bible study with Tanus, and learned powerful Bible principles. Most of all, I learned to apply these principles. I finally felt strong enough to gain full-time employment. The voice of the Lord divided the flames of the fire.

Although Gary Jr. and I got kicked out of our apartment, I was able to rent a small room for five hundred dollars a month. I was starting to feel more confident about myself. The more I was reintroduced to my creator, Jesus Christ, the more clarity I received in my daily walk. I started to fall in love with Tanus.

I loved him for taking the time to hear my story and help me fight the demons. As time passed by, Tanus and I realized that God did not send him into my life in order to be in a relationship. God, who is almighty, may use anyone or anything in order to accomplish His divine purpose. Our plans may not be what His will is for our lives. Once I fully rededicated my life to Jesus Christ, the demons stopped harassing me. All that I lost, Christ began to give back. After I was delivered, I learned how to walk in freedom.

One Sunday morning I decided to visit my home church. As I stepped into the church, I heard the choir singing the song that I used to lead, as a teen-ager, *Try Me One More Time.* "Try me one more time. One more time. Give me a chance to know you. Try me one more time. Give me a chance to show you. I will live holy, like you want me to, if you try me one more time." Tears began to fill my eyes.

As the choir members noticed me coming into the sanctuary, they all ran up to me and embraced me. The choir director gave me the microphone. She wanted the Sabrina Matheson who was snatched from the fire to declare that Jesus Christ is Lord, before the congregation. I took the mike, and screamed, "Jesus Christ is Lord." I proceeded to lead the choir, singing *Try Me One More Time.*

> Try me one more time, Lord
> Give me a chance just to know you,
> Try me one more time,
> Lord give me a chance to show you.
> I will live holy, like you want me to,
> If you try me one more time. . . .

Only the love of Christ can move true Christians to allow themselves to be used by Christ in order to free the captives, and snatch other souls from the fire. The fire is real, the fire is dangerous, but Jesus Christ, the almighty, is all powerful.

www.ingramcontent.com/pod-product-compliance
Lightning Source LLC
Chambersburg PA
CBHW031858090426
42741CB00005B/550